Sus<

Thank-

Natalie

MW00331057

THE SHORT SIDE OF PARADISE

NATALIE
BEAUMONT

THE SHORT SIDE
OF PARADISE

A Memoir

Full Court Press
Englewood Cliffs, New Jersey

First Edition

Copyright © 2015 by Natalie Beaumont

Published in the United States of America
by Full Court Press, 601 Palisade Avenue
Englewood Cliffs, NJ 07632
fullcourtpressnj.com

ISBN 978-1-938812-50-7
Library of Congress Control No. 2015931774

*Editing and Book Design by Barry Sheinkopf
for Bookshapers (bookshapers.com)*

Cover Art courtesy istockphoto.com

Colophon by Liz Sedlack

To my son, ANTHONY FRANCIS CALIFANO

my pride and joy, who inadvertently shared
most of my story, for better or for worse.

Acknowledgments

Thanks to:

My high school typing teacher, whose name escapes me.

My parents, grandparents, and great grandfather, for getting me hooked on letter-writing and telling anecdotes.

My high school English teacher, Mrs. Edith Persehouse, who encouraged me after reading my first two unassigned pieces and told me I should continue to study poetry;

Barry Sheinkopf of The Writing Center, in Englewood Cliffs, New Jersey, for his encouragement when I couldn't find anything to be encouraged about, and for his creativity, versatility, generosity, and kindness, not to mention his vast array of knowledge in so many areas.

Table of Contents

PROPHECY

There is a hole inside my personality.
Sometime, somewhere in my growing up,
Something got undernourished, wounded.
And now, to try to open and heal it—
it's so sensitive that,
if not opened right, I'll panic
and blame all those in my way.
I'm like a bird with a broken wing healed over,
But the infection festers beneath
and is poisoning my blood.
To be cured, it must be opened;
that will hurt, unless it's done
so I can't feel the poison drain out.
Otherwise, it will infect the whole of me—
my body, energies, my being.
Sometimes I think it's healing, then realize
the curse of the infection is still there.
If it's torn open, I will die.
If it's scratched out, I will be impaired for life.
If it's drained and cleared, I'll live.

CITY BOY, SUBURBS GIRL

GIRL FROM THE SUBURBS trying out social work after college, and a street-smart high school drop-out and gang kid city boy, met at work in St. Luke's Hospital. He brought medical charts to the various departments; she had an office in Social Services. She was me.

"Good morning, Miss Beaumont," he'd say. Such dark hair and blue, blue eyes looking right at me!

"Good morning, Larry."

Everyone liked Larry. He worked hard and was friendly; he even knew two of my relatives: Dr. Will Norton, the diabetic doctor, my mother's first cousin; and Dottie Revelle, my father's cousin, who worked in the clinic.

On our first date, Larry invited me to see *West Side Story*. *His* story, he told me. He brought me a teddy bear when he came to pick me up. Nobody had ever done that before!

On another date, he took me to see a boxing match in Madison Square Garden: Emile Griffith vs. Peret. Emile Griffith, strong as a black brick wall, battered Peret until he was out cold and taken to the hospital in a coma; about three days later, Peret died. Larry was apologetic, but I was eighteen and couldn't really imagine what that battering might have felt like; I couldn't relate to fighting sports outside of football and ice hockey. Larry's father, Ralph, liked to watch the "wrasslin'," and I, upon watching the "wrasslers" once with their long-haired wigs and pot-bellied bodies, said, "That's not real! He hit his back with a flat arm! That's just for show!"

Larry put his finger to his lips, as if to say, "Don't tell! He likes to *think* it's real."

Larry (whose mother, Mary Sweeney, was Irish) took me to the St. Patrick's Day parade on Fifth Avenue in March 1962. There I met Larry's brother Frank and his buddy Eddie Hogan, who lived above Larry on the fifth floor of his walk-up apartment on 109th between Amsterdam and Columbus. Eddie's mother, Wanda, was a bit alcoholic and flaky; his father, Johnny, was a good man who worked but suffered from ulcers—no wonder, since Wanda slept until 4:00 p.m. and did the laundry at 4:00 a.m. Eddie had the brogue down pat, though. One of his bits was to imitate his father when he couldn't find his false teeth: "Bejasus, wher'er me whoorin' chompers? Did ye trow 'em in the garbage, Wanda, win ye was too goddamn potted ta see 'em?"

I invited Larry to dinner at my parents' home in the house I grew up in, in Englewood, or "Jersey," as New Yorkers called it. They found him personable and charming and said he was so adaptable. If my father quoted P. G. Wodehouse, Larry would remember the quote and use it on his friends. He'd change his style of speaking to resemble that of his future father-in-law, though, returning home from "Jersey," he'd call his best friend: "Ed! How ya doin', pal?"

At this time of early romance, Larry's mother, who had spent eight years at Rockland State Hospital for some kind of breakdown caused by, Larry thought, the change of life, returned home. Molly was a short, stout woman with a high forehead under short white hair and a ruddy complexion, who had come from Ireland at the age of eighteen and had never met some of her seventeen siblings but followed her sister, Aunt Catherine, who showed up sometimes. Catherine was taller but was similarly white-haired, and disdained using a vacuum cleaner on the dusty floor when a perfectly effective broom could do the job; I found out when I brought over my new, wonderful Electrolux vacuum cleaner to 102 West 109th. Larry's father, Ralph, was a quiet man, gentle, sweet, and unassuming. Larry and Frank had lived with Ralph and their uncle Otto, a tailor, while Molly was at Rockland State.

Here was an adjustment for all concerned. Life with the men was easygoing and companionable. The return of Molly presented a challenge, and she would receive visits occasionally from her friend Mae Sugrue, a feisty lady who, if she'd had better language skills, might have gotten into politics. A member of the Grey Panthers she was, and proud of it.

On occasion, after seeing a show, Larry and I would have a drink at a piano bar with Larry's cousin Conrad (Connie) Monjoy, who played piano. Connie had voiced his misgivings over moving back to New York after spending some years in Los Angeles.

PERHAPS THAT WAS AN OMEN, for, in the not-too-distant future, we would put our things in storage and fly the friendly skies to San Francisco—I, now Mrs. Califano, to work, allowing Larry to get his G.E.D. It was quite an adventure or, put in another way, my attempt to escape the unexplained but implied expectations of my former suburban cocoon; his to leave a tough environment where many of his old buddies hit on him for drug money, he to go to a community college that he had read all about. It's not a surprise that, when someone has grown up in a tough neighborhood in the inner city and goes to a place where there are palm trees, warm sun, and beaches, they would want to stay. Kosher hot dogs with mustard and sauerkraut can't hold a torch to that, or roasted chestnuts and huge pretzels, or Coney Island! And Larry had a wise philosophy: "If you're going to be poor, be poor in California, not in New York."

We were married at the First Presbyterian Church in Englewood, where I had been baptized and confirmed. Larry had been raised Catholic, and Molly was concerned about his not being married in the Catholic Church. Larry resented the Catholic Church. He said they wanted him to believe things he didn't believe, and the Christian Brothers at the Rice Catholic School exercised the tough, punitive style that employed corporal punishment. He told the story of his friend, Thomas Watters: When the brother said, "I don't want to hear a peep out of anyone!" Watters had whispered, "Peep!" in the ensuing silence. He had been hung by his jacket on a coat hook but dared to laugh for all to hear! Later he became a junkie, and Larry said that, if he turned sideways, you couldn't see him. One of the things he had done was steal his mother's new washing machine to pay for junk. He was in and out of rehab, and, many years later, got clean and married a nurse but, sadly, fell from a tree and crushed his spinal chord, rendering him immobile. Larry's friend John Flaherty, who went to Los Angeles and got into acting, told that sad story.

When my best friend Penny and I graduated from college—she from Wheaton, and I from St. Lawrence—we found an apartment on Haven Avenue, near Columbia Presbyterian Hospital. Penny went to Columbia Teacher's College and worked briefly as a temp during the time that I was dating Larry. One night she came home from a party and told me she was going to California the next morning! Her friends had convinced her that it would be a great adventure to drive across the country to San Francisco. So she had one night to pack. I later packed a trunk with the rest of Penny's belongings and sent it off when she had an address. And off they went. I was making enough money to cover the rent; once married, Larry moved in.

FOR MOLLY'S SAKE, Larry and I did speak to a very nice Cuban priest in the 109th Street neighborhood. He told us that, if we married in the Catholic Church, we would be married forever. But in talking to him, I explained that I was an active member of the Presbyterian Church, attending church regularly and singing in the choir; if we married in the Catholic Church without Larry being an active member, I would have no incentive to convert. I also wanted to know whether, if we married in the Presbyterian Church, Larry's Catholic friends would be "allowed" to attend. No one seemed to have a real answer to the question, so I decided to write Pope John. Larry called it my "Dear John" letter.

It was forwarded to the Archdiocese of New York, and, some time later, I received a letter from a Monsignor O'Brien, who acknowledged receipt of my letter and gave a phone number to call

me to even mention anything, but she had been curious and asked).

The result was that I was terminated, but very graciously—her father offering to give me a good reference. I can still picture her, lean, light-haired, looking to the side on Broadway, pulling me as she noticed the change in the direction of the traffic faster than I noticed the light changing!

When Larry told the Director of Social Services that I wasn't working, she called me into her office and offered me a job as a case aide at Woman's Hospital, where I would be working with mostly terminal cancer patients in the city ward as opposed to the private wards. I was happy to be working there. Death had not become a reality to me, but the appreciation of every kindness they received made a deep impression on me. I would have loved to sing to them, for some reason. I also liked and respected my co-workers, the doctors and the staff. But that was when I already knew we'd be going to California.

In preparing to leave, we packed and moved all the things we owned to my parents' house on Sherwood Place, including a comfortable double bed from Macy's Mom had given us for a wedding present, as well as the two silver coffee/tea trays, the twelve casserole dishes, family silver or plate silverware, as well as the stainless steel cutlery from the Side Door, a nice gift store in Englewood where I had worked briefly when in high school.

Larry's friend Joe McGovern put the bed in storage in New York, to be sent when we called. I wrote my cousin John Reynolds and asked him if we could visit in Santa Barbara, and we also contacted Penny in San Francisco to see if we could spend a few days there before taking a bus to Santa Barbara. Then it was time for us to embark on our new life!

SAN FRANCISCO

Penny and her roommate, Pat Johnson (PJ), whose father had been my pediatrician, picked us up at the San Francisco Airport and brought us to their apartment. Pat, who came from an athletic family, taught physical education at one of the local schools; and Penny was teaching at a private school.

As always, she knew all the interesting places we should visit and how to get there. We went to Sausalito, to Golden Gate Park, to Market Street to browse, and to the Haight-Ashbury, hippie haven, and of course we took our hostesses to dinner. We spent our final night with another Englewood and Dwight School chum, Janie Roberts, now a nurse, and her husband Dr. David Johnson, an intern at one of the hospitals.

Janie prepared a lovely dinner of meat loaf, salad, whipped potatoes, and, over dinner and wine, we heard the *news*: A fire had been ravaging Santa Barbara—the Coyote Fire, the flames of which sometimes jumped over some houses and trees with the wind and landed in other unexpected places. It was in the papers, on the radio and TV, with countless homes destroyed. One man, apparently, had taken a hose up to his roof and watered it down, thereby saving the house! The next morning we were to take a bus from Janie and David's to the San Francisco Bus Terminal and trek down to Santa Barbara, not knowing if John and Dottie and their five children had a house!

Once out of San Francisco, looking out the windows of the bus, we saw brown hills and a lot of open land along the freeway dotted with some California scrub oak. We stopped in Santa Maria, heard more talk, and saw headlines and pictures of the ferocious fire. Not knowing what to expect, we only knew that John would be picking us up. What a different landscape! As we got nearer to Santa Barbara, we observed all the Spanish red-tiled houses, the palm trees everywhere, and at times the crisp, cool, metallic blue of the Pacific Ocean.

The Santa Barbara Bus Depot was small, and there, waiting for us, was my good-looking, tall cousin John, blue eyes and fair skin in place, and his short, bubbly wife, Dottie. They drove us to their home on Park Lane in Montecito, next to the Montecito Country Club, and there, looking across the street, I could see the charred grass burned when the wind had blown flames over an untouched field, only to burn the lot across the street from their expansive, Spanish-style home. We put our suitcases in our room and came down to meet five children: Johnny, Dottie's oldest from her first marriage, and his wife Pam, pretty, blue-eyed, with an oval-shaped face and fine, long brown hair, who loved being married; then Courtney ("Corky"), also from Dottie's first marriage, and resembled Dottie; then Sharon, the tall, statuesque, artistic, talented, and rebellious daughter from Dottie's second disastrous marriage; then Monica, named after John's sister, affectionately called "Aunt Monkey," (Aunt Monkey had studied lactation at Columbia Presbyterian Hospital); and Pierce, the youngest of Dottie and John's two. To celebrate our arrival, we all went to Joe's Café on State Street, the main thoroughfare in Santa Barbara proper, a darkish but small, cozy place known for its sourdough French bread and butter, salsa, and sour cream, along with your standard hamburgers, steak, salads, and drinks. While dining, one could also look at all the photos and caricatures of movie stars on the walls. Dottie and John had a tradition of going to Joe's on Sunday nights with their friends, and also enjoyed frequent lunches there. A few doors down stood the Mission Theater, which usually showed movies in Spanish, as opposed to the Spanish-style Granada Theater farther up State Street, or the Lobero, on Anacapa and Santa Barbara Streets.

I had met Dottie once in Englewood when she was first married to John, and though I liked her a lot, I was upset then with John, who had given me "lumps" for something I had done; when he apologized, I had slapped him, and he'd given me lumps again. I was doubly humiliated because we had guests over. I went upstairs to my bedroom closet and stayed there for the rest of the evening.

LUMPS ARE A MEAN FORM OF PUNISHMENT. John would grab you and feel the area of bone between the two muscles on your upper arm. Then he would hit that area with the knuckle of his thumb a given number of times, depending on the severity of the punishment. It hurt. A lot. And it was humiliating, especially as I got older. It had started because he spent vacations with us when a student at Choate School and later at Yale. My brother, sister, and I used to bug him when he was studying or drawing. We learned he did this with his and Dottie's kids as well. But we all liked him, since he would tell us ghost stories, which he also did with his kids, and, always an artist, draw pictures of us at different times.

John was quite reserved, but Dottie was spunky, playful, and gregarious, which John liked. She appreciated his "courage" in marrying her with three children from two previous marriages. After our dinner at Joe's, Dottie and I, both in high heels, had a race to the car to see who could run faster in them.

They were wonderful hosts. Since I had my driver's license, they let me use one of their three cars any time. On several occasions, I took Larry and the kids horseback riding, though once, Pierce was so obnoxious that I pulled him out of the car and let him walk the rest of the way home. Larry, coming from where he did, used to say he'd love to beat the shit out of the spoiled little rich-kid bastard, but as it turned out, Pierce acquired his own burdens as time went on. Monica, about thirteen, used to think she was a horse and was good, when on all fours, at neighing and throwing up her legs into the air. Sharon, a wonderful swimmer and dancer, tended to hang out with a tough classmate, Cindy, who smoked and did drugs and wasn't allowed over; sometimes Sharon was grounded for being out with her. Courtney resembled her mother: She was attractive and outgoing and found humor in many situations. She had a boyfriend whom she liked a lot, though eventually they broke up.

SINCE DOTTIE WORKED THREE DAYS A WEEK at an adoption agency, each child was assigned to cook dinner one night a week. It was quite interesting (and I wished I could have had such an experience growing up rather than waiting, grouchy and tired, for my mother to get home and have her two martinis before we could eat). Larry and I both gained weight while we were there.

John loved history and enjoyed talking about how he had

learned the subject, which I liked, because I was afraid of it. "Take a period in time," he would say, "and then consider what was going on in different parts of the world in that period, so you can see relationships between countries in the same eras." This made a lot of sense to me, since I had trouble memorizing an event and a matching date. John was also an artist; he had drawn and painted for as long as we had known him, and he had his pictures on his walls, many of his family and of Santa Barbara in general.

"I spent some time committed just to painting," he told me at one time, "but I began drinking earlier and earlier in the day. So to break that habit, I started to help Johnny (his step-son) at the Montecito Hardware Store." More power to him. It wasn't the last important decision he made for himself. The Montecito Hardware store lent itself to many jokes during Sunday drinks and dinner, such as, "How many screws did you get this week, John?" They were a hilarious group with their friends, be it in the hardware store or spotting nude bathers when on outings on John's boat.

All the Reynoldses liked Larry, and Larry liked being there, not just in their expansive Spanish-style home, but in Santa Barbara, where the sun shone bright, the beach was a few stone throws away, and many of the streets were lined with palm trees. John told me that, as an artist, when he first came to Santa Barbara he had hated the bright sun and missed the more subtle shades of color one sees on the East Coast, but after a while, he came to appreciate the brightness, and he changed his style of painting numerous times over the years to accommodate it. He didn't sell his paintings, just gave them to his friends as gifts. Fortunately for him, he was independently wealthy thanks to his mother, Ursula Carr

(Dr. George Carr having been her third husband), from whom he inherited a beach cottage the next town south, in Santa Claus, Carpinteria, just south of Montecito and Summerland. It still seems incongruous that one can drive down to Santa Claus and see, in the middle of ocean, sand, palm trees, and sun, a Santa in the chimney of a restaurant called The Reindeer Room, to the roof of which Santa's reindeer are also attached!

MY FATHER HAD GIVEN ME THE NAME, address, and phone number of one of his best friends from his years growing up in Wilkes-Barre, Pennsylvania, "Bo" Dougher. He and his wife invited Larry and me to a party they had in their home in the San Roque area of Santa Barbara, where they lived. One of his three daughters lived across the road in a matching house. I had met Bo's mother several times when my Aunt Elsie, Dad's sister, took me to visit in Wilkes-Barre — a very tall, thin, light-skinned woman — and noticed the blood veins on her forehead. Her son Bo and one of her granddaughters, Peggy, had the same height, thinness, and fair skin, I observed, and later I met Peggy.

When Larry and I arrived *chez* Dougher, Bo told me that he remembered my father as a belligerent pacifist: "Your father was passionately opposed to war, but if you argued with him you were likely to get a poke in the nose. But when the Japanese bombed Pearl Harbor and I was stationed overseas, I received a telegram from Butts asking, *Where do I enlist?* And that is how Bo Dougher introduced me to all his friends at his party!

Larry matched Bo's story with one of his own: When Eddie Hopkins, Larry's best friend, came to our wedding reception (not the wedding, as it was in a protestant church and he was slated to be married in the Catholic Church), he needed directions to get back onto the New Jersey Turnpike. When they approached my father to get this information, Dad replied, cheerfully, "Elementary, my dear Watson!"

When Eddie and Larry walked to Ed's car, he asked Larry, "What did he say about Watson?" Dad often used to quote from his favorite authors, which created much colorful language in his conversations.

LARRY NEEDED A JOB before taking the placement test at Santa Barbara City College, and he found one at I. Magnin, on State Street, not far from Joe's Cafe.

We went shopping for cars and found a Volkswagen Beetle at a VW place on Chapala Street, one block over from State. Neither of us had credit, so this was our first attempt at having it. While Larry was working, I looked for apartments and found a one-bedroom in a charming building with four of them in a small, two-story house, another house on the side, and two-story house in back, connected to six garages. So after spending three months with Dottie and John, we moved in to 410 West Sola Street.

My favorite features of our upstairs apartment were the back-door stairs and the clothesline and pulley attached to the outside wall and the house in back. Remembering the days when my mother hung the laundry to dry in the '30s, '40s, and '50s, and the fresh smell of the clothes, sheets, and towels, I used the clothesline enthusiastically. And they dried so quickly!

Until we had all our things, including the many wedding presents shipped, we had two each of our plates, dishes, and silverware, and that was fine with me.

THE FIRST PERSON I MET other than the Reynoldses was Tom Mooney. Tom worked in an imported-candies store in the El Paseo, a charming, Spanish-style block off State Street where one could walk or sit at tables in a square area, with numerous shops and restaurants around. I went into the candy store, looking for some white chocolate to give my cousins as a thank-you token. Tom loved talking to people. He had the gift of the gab, as the Irish say. He was tall, with longish brown hair in a pony-tail and a thick mustache, and was fairly lean and athletic looking in his button-down plaid shirt, dark jeans, and boots. And he was most generous with his samples! I couldn't help wondering whether he made any money at his job, though I am sure he had a good time. Every so often I would stop in, and occasionally saw his wife, Doris, and their youngest child, Erin.

When I told Tom that I was looking for a temporary job, he gave me a lead: a Los Angeles artist, Perli Pelzig, had designed a tapestry of the *Seven Fruits of the Bible*. A tapestry maker, Nora Noel, needed people to weave the design of the tapestry on a loom set up in her garage. I went to Nora's, and she showed me how to weave the threads into the design in each section. There were about six others working on this project. Larry and I had moved into our apartment on Sola Street by then, and I used to enjoy walking across town, past Milpas (corn-field) Street, and spend the day weaving and talking with the different personalities engaged in the project.

Doris Mooney was one of the workers, and Tom when able;

Erin came and played with a child in the neighborhood. Doris told us that the two little girls had a fight one day; the little black girl said to Erin, "You stupid nigger!" to which Erin countered,

"You stupid fatso rat-fink!"

I remained friends with several of those people, especially Doris and Tom Mooney, and Pauline, who, after the tapestry was done, joined me in a job as motel maid in a motel near the beach.

I was fired, since I couldn't get the beds perfect enough (they had to be AAA approved) and got exhausted doing that tedious, heavy work all day. (Paule, shorter and less athletic than I, was promoted to chief motel maid!) While working there, though, I wondered what Uncle Buzz would have thought, or said, had he stayed there and I had been the motel maid in charge of cleaning his room. I could only hope he'd have given me a large tip!

Pauline was spending time with one of the other tapestry workers, Jon, who was ten years her junior, tall, blond, with one silver earring, and somewhat recalcitrant with Pauline. When she asked him several times to look at something on the tapestry and he ignored her, I said in a loud voice, "Jon, get your ass over there!" and over he went, immediately.

They stayed together for awhile, and we went over for several delicious meals Paule cooked, but later they split up. Pauline started teaching cooking classes for the Adult Education Program in Santa Barbara and later married a very nice man, and more suitable than Jon would ever have been.

Nora and her husband Bob, a professor at the University of California, Santa Barbara, split up, and I would see him ten years later in a therapy group.

When the tapestry was completed, it was sent to Perli Pelzig's studio in Los Angeles, and we all carpooled there for a champagne celebration and the whole of *The Seven Fruits of the Bible* was displayed under lights in his large studio. I rode in Doris and Tom's car, and we found our way to the studio in the middle of the sprawling city. The highway and street signs were more visible there than in Bergen County, New Jersey, I couldn't help noticing.

The most memorable thing about the affair was that I passed out. I might have had about one-fourth of my champagne and was talking to several people. The next thing I knew, I was on the floor, encircled by six faces. Everyone was concerned, and Perli himself invited me to stay there for the night if I needed to. I was seated in a chair, and a discussion ensued about what could have happened. The answer was clear: I hadn't had lunch. Drinking champagne — or anything — is not wise when one hasn't eaten, a lesson I learned first-hand through that, and other, less graphic experiences. I had no fear of getting home, and one such drama is enough. When I later told Dottie about this incident, she suggested that I might have had low blood sugar, which she had, a prediction that turned out to be true.

Mrs. Beaumont the Sleuth and the Missing Bed

When all of our wedding gifts had arrived in our upstairs one-bedroom apartment at 410 West Sola Street, the one thing that failed to arrive was the comfortable, firm-mattressed Macy's bed Mom had given us. Larry's friend, Joe McGovern, had picked it up and taken it to one of his storage places in the city, waiting for Larry to let him know when it could be sent. Larry had called Joe, and Joe had said he'd take it to my parents, who would have it shipped to us. A week passed. Then two weeks. Three weeks. Mom reported that no bed had arrived. Larry called Joe several times. There was no answer. Mom called us and asked Larry where he might be tracked down. Well, there was Fell's Bar on Amsterdam and 106th, and (Paddy) Murphy's Bar on the corner of Amsterdam and 109th, and about six other possibilities. Various kinds of business were transacted in the bars in the neighborhood. Mom got the names and looked them up or called information for the numbers. Her inquiries went something like:

"Murphy's!"

"I am trying to locate Mr. Joe McGovern."

"He ain't here, ma'am."

"May I leave him a message?"

"Sure, ma'am. What is it?"

"Please tell him to call Larry Califano's *mother-in-law!* At Lowell 8-0202."

"Yes, ma'am, I'll relay that to him."

"Thank you very much. Good evening," she concluded in her snippiest voice.

She kept calling the bars, and one evening yet more weeks later, reached Joe McGovern himself:

"Hallo, Joe here."

"This is Larry Califano's *mother-in-law.* Where is the bed you were to bring here?"

"Uh, well, ma'am, it's in one of my storage places in the city.

We gotta lotta furniture comin' in, so I couldn't locate it right away, ma'am."

"It has to be brought here *immediately*," she declared in her You'd-better-watch-out-I-mean-business tone. "You have already been paid to do so."

"Ah, well, ma'am, I'll try to get it there by the weekend— maybe Saturday."

"See that you do. Do you have the correct address?"

"Yes, ma'am. Link gave it to me."

"I will expect it on Saturday. Good evening."

THE BED NEVER CAME. A year or so later, when Larry and I came to visit, he took a side trip to his old neighborhood and happened into Murphy's Bar with his best friend Eddie Hopkins, where who should he see but none other than Joe McGovern.

"Ey, man, how ya doin', pal?" said Larry.

"Ey, Link, you're lookin' good. How's California treatin' youse?"

"If you're gonna be poor, be poor in California. It's a lot warmer there in the winter. Sooo, I hear ya talked to my mother-in-law."

"Jeeziz, Link, she's a bitch."

"Yah, ya don' wanna mess with her. What happened to the bed, anyway?

"Well, Link, I dunno. I looked for it but never found it. If it wasn't labeled right, one of my workers might have taken it for a walk."

"It was a pretty nice bed. No hard feelings, though."

So the saga went. Mom had made a heroic effort at tracking down the Macy's bed and enjoying the drama of it. I'm just as glad she didn't go looking for Joe in person. Suffice it to say, I was disappointed not to get the bed, but since our apartment was furnished, we just settled for the one that was there, inferior as it was.

SANTA BARBARA CITY COLLEGE

Larry took the placement test at Santa Barbara City College (SBCC), located on Cliff Drive and one of my favorite spots, on a hill overlooking the cobalt-blue Pacific. The offices and classrooms stood on the top of the hill; a field, stadium, a track, an amphitheater, and several parking lots lay below.

In the meantime, I interviewed and got a job working in the business office at St. Francis Hospital, a small Catholic facility on the east side of Santa Barbara and situated on a higher hill, and a twenty-minute walk from our apartment.

I enjoyed walking to work, and it was especially pleasant to do so early in the morning when I worked from 7:00 a.m. to 3:30 p.m., looking at the sunbeams shining through the palms in Alameda Park on the way to the hospital. I had to learn the switchboard, admitting, counting the cash at the beginning and end of the day, and making sure the books balanced. I had never used an adding machine, but I learned how there and enjoyed it, though it was always stressful when the books didn't balance and we had to figure out where the errors were. Some of the office staff were not patient when teaching new people, and I was offended several times, but later on I was the one who taught the new people and, having learned Spanish, helped explain to Spanish-speaking employees what was being deducted from their salaries.

In the meantime, Larry needed to pass a math and an English class to get his G.E.D. and then took classes required for obtaining an A.A. degree, with the option of going to a four-year college or going to work thereafter. He earned a bit of money working in the work-study program at the college, helping the custodial staff put in plants, remove garbage, and generally keep the place clean. And he had papers to write. As I had brought along my trusty typewriter, I could help, and did, but there arose a problem: Larry, who worked very hard at a job, had difficulty in the less structured role of a student. And writing papers did not come easy to him then. He read a lot, and understood the material and could talk about it. But write a paper, with footnotes? Difficult. He sat down on the couch while I sat at my typewriter. He thought of things to say about the subject. But then he'd get a different idea and want to change what I had typed. This did not work. He got his papers written, but I don't remember how. I think he got help at the college's reading study skills center.

This was a difficult time for Larry, who, except for a brief stint in the U.S. Marines, had not finished school and had not really been outside of New York. So it was a huge adjustment, and I am sure he felt at loose ends at this time. I, anticipating a new adventure in a new place, thought supporting him find a new life path was very exciting. I sometimes said to myself what I had learned in school: We have been given much by society and we must give back to pay our debt to society. So marrying a man who was nice to me, and helping him get on was my way of repaying that debt. It was a good fit, or so I thought at the time.

One afternoon when Larry came back from school, he told me he had lost his wedding ring. He was talking to a girl at the beach and nervously playing with his ring. He'd dropped it in the sand. As he dug for it, it'd sunk deeper, and he couldn't find it. Well, that was that.

DOTTIE AND JOHN WERE VERY GOOD to us and always invited us to come for dinner on holidays and at other times as well. The Beaumont holidays at 170 Sherwood, the old homestead, were festive but involved; among the grown-ups, a good amount of drinking took place, and often I ended up feeling guilty because I was bored and ate too much. My father had developed a technique for cutting back on the booze; as the gracious host and bartender, he would have one whiskey and then switch to bouillon, thus avoiding a hangover. The men liked to congregate in the kitchen and pantry while he worked his cocktail magic. However, I did not like to see my mother get loaded, and loaded she got. I went out with friends as soon as I could after the meal. In Santa Barbara, I was happy to work on holidays in my new life, thereby missing the overeating and drinking *chez* Reynolds. Larry would go to the Reynoldses' earlier and enjoy the scene, and I would come after a quiet day at work.

WE HAD SOME INTERESTING NEIGHBORS. Don Robertson lived on the first floor in a charming apartment, which he kept a mess. He was fat—really fat—and fancied himself a folk singer. He didn't have very many upper front teeth; those two factors belied his self-image as a sexy stud. He would often practice his guitar, playing and singing his heart out, not in the shower, but on the pot. He worked as a bar tender in a small, dark bar off of lower State Street and fancied himself a freethinker and hippie. Our landlady, Mrs. Blanche McElhaney, eventually evicted him.

In the brown house across the driveway lived Lydia and Mike Meissner and Jill, their two-year-old girl. They were from Germany. Mike worked for the City of Santa Barbara as an engineer. He was an outdoorsman who enjoyed hunting, and Lydia knew how to tenderize and cook venison and rabbit, among other things. She was a fine cook and could also sew. She made suits for Mike and all of Jill's clothes. We enjoyed their company and were sorry when they moved; they later divorced, though Lydia remained my friend for many years.

The apartment below us was usually rented by students; we didn't know the people in the house behind us, but when they moved out after about two years, we moved into the little two-bedroom house, and I could still use the pulley to hang my laundry from the roof.

Larry made friends with another student at City College, who worked at Safeway, about three blocks away from us. Kent was a pleasant, nice-looking young man and often came to our door with day-old bread and cake from Safeway. He was of medium height and a blue-eyed blond, and we enjoyed his company a lot. We were sorry to see him leave when he enlisted and was sent to Viet Nam. We later saw in the news that he had been killed.

Another couple we got to know were Carol and John, who rented a small, charming house up Castillo Street, which ran perpendicular to Sola. There was a creek behind their house that gave the place a romantic touch. Carol had the blond hair, fair skin, blue eyes, and oval face of the women painted by Flemish artists. She usually wore long dresses, and she kept their home neat, clean, and orderly. John was tall and had long graying hair, and he sported a long beard, the center of which he braided. It didn't appeal to me, but I liked him and was impressed that he could read, write, and speak one of the Chinese languages. Carol baked her own bread and made jams and jellies, all of which she took to the beach on Sunday afternoons to sell at the arts and crafts market. On one occasion, she told us that an older couple walking by her spot and observing her long dress, long hair, and bread had remarked to her husband, "I'd hate to see the kitchen that bread came out of." It reminded me of my father's comment, "You want to go to California, where all the vegetarians and religious fanatics live?"

DREAMS, DAYDREAMS, VISIONS, IMAGININGS: LIFE AND DEATH

ANY YEARS AGO, when I was in my early teens, I wrote a short piece that turned out to be prophetic. I wrote that there was a poison in my body and psyche that, if not removed at some point, even if it meant losing something major, would destroy me, and that this poison was slowly but insidiously invading my system, working to such an end.

I found that piece not long ago, remembered writing it, and, as a result of some medical and psychological issues then challenging me, knew it to be true. On the other hand, I was also conscious of what caused me to feel healthy and in balance.

One of the most healing times in my life came in 1999, when I went on a folk dance tour to Tunisia with Jim Gold. It was the most unusual place I have ever been to. The major highlight was our camel ride in the Sahara Desert. It was noon—not a good time to go for an outing in the desert sun. But we wore long pants, long-sleeved shirts, and head scarves for protection against the pounding heat. My clothes were loose, and a warm wind blew through them; I sat on a large cushion and held on to a wooden frame where my water bottle rested. The sun, the sand, the rocking of the camel's gait, the hot breeze, and the stretch of desert. . .what a speck we are in eternity! Seeing shepherds and goat herders living as they had since before Christ emphasized that notion. Many times in the intervening years, I have imagined that sun healing me inside and out, sterilizing the poison that was trying to pollute me.

Nine years later, I was dying from a blockage caused by Crohn's disease, and I literally did not want to live any more with the evil claw of Crohn's wrecking my body. I could not function; I could not remember what meds to take; I knew only that I needed to hand out copies of personal contacts before going to Mount Sinai Hospital to die or have the poison removed. My dear friend Charlotte made it her mission to get me to the specialist in New York in the morning, then back to Englewood for a CD of my latest cat scan, and then back to Mount Sinai for surgery the next day. She was with me from 9:00 a.m. to 6:00 p.m. and then, after I was admitted, went to a planning board meeting! And at last I could lie there and go to sleep.

In surgery, I was aware only of some presence. I thought it was God, but it gave no indication that I would live or die. At one point I heard a strong voice say, "*Open your eyes. Focus.*" Some time later, I woke up and saw the pink sky of dawn out my window, over the city's skyscrapers.

No doubt, the surgeon or anesthesiologist had spoken to me, but I thought it was God telling me to keep my own focus and pay-attention to what was essential in my life.

That was in 2008. Two years later, I have a kind of energy I haven't had in years. However, I have had other dreams which seemed uncanny:

One midsummer night In 2000, I was startled from a deep sleep when I heard a very strong voice call out, *"Natalie!"* I awoke with a start and briefly sensed a presence. It sounded like the voice of a boyfriend I'd had in Santa Barbara, whom I had broken up with. The following February, I learned through a mutual friend that he'd had to have a leg amputated from mid-thigh because of a cancerous cyst that had been found—a previous cyst had been removed, but a biopsy had not been taken, and this cancer had metastasized very quickly. I did not wish that on anyone and so called to express my condolences.

As it turned out, we made amends, and I was with him when he breathed his last breath.

There have been other dreams that I wonder about. In 2004, I was having a severe flare-up of Crohn's; I had to be hospitalized for dehydration; my electrolytes needed to be re-balanced through intravenous potassium. (At first, the nurse put the potassium IV rather than the solution closer to my vein. The full strength of the potassium caused me to feel that my arm was on fire. I learned to remind the nurse to put the saline closer to the vein and the potassium on the lower, distal line.) I remembered that my mother had worked in that hospital for thirty-five years. One morning, a woman from the lab came in to take my blood. I mentioned Mom's involvement with the lab; she looked at my chart and proceeded to name all the people who had worked with her. It was comforting, for some reason. I had just read from a book of meditations someone had given me that all things in the past would be washed clean and purified. That night, I dreamed that I was reaching out to my mother, and she to me, while pure, clear water passed between us. On another night I dreamed that I was standing in front of an arch framing a partially open doorway, and that a bright light was coming through it. Such unexpected images we get in our dreams!

THE YEAR BEFORE MY MOTHER DIED, my father called to tell me she had been admitted to ICU (in the same hospital she had worked in for all those thirty-five years), and that her prognosis was uncertain. I felt panic and an urgent need to see her before she died. Then I felt a peaceful sensation and a closeness to her, as if everything would be all right. Fortunately, I got there in time to see her come home. I learned how to treat her bed sores, but mainly I had the chance to affirm what our relationship was: one of deep love and respect as well as one in which a thick psychological wall blocked any rapport or communication.

Although my family was well read and enjoyed theater and music, I was not encouraged much in those areas, though my mother once told me I had a good stage presence. Our relatives who were inclined to the stage were considered "charming but unstable." So what I loved most was not important. I enjoyed the music of Edith Piaf, Yves Montand, Theodore Bikel, Jaqueline Francois, Jacques Brel, the Singing Nun, Fauré, opera, oldies but goodies, and most Broadway shows; I wanted to sing them all. I wanted to sing with Paul Robeson, Harry Belafonte, and on and on. One morning when living in Santa Barbara, I was walking to work at 6:30 a.m. and heard a voice whisper my name very softly—once it was Edith Piaf; another time it was my grandmother. Of course it was all my imagination, but what is that really? Employed as a social worker at St. Luke's Hospital in New York, I always wanted to sing to the patients on my caseload, all of them female terminal cancer patients. Later, in Santa Barbara, I did sing in retirement homes.

I HAD TWO VIETNAMESE STUDENTS in my ESL class in Santa Barbara in the mid-seventies. They had never met, but they had both had the same dream.: They were in Vietnam, in the middle of chaos and disaster. An angel, or someone, appeared and asked them, *"Where are you going, and what are you doing?"* They said they didn't know, and this person, or apparition, told them to follow her; they came to a quiet, peaceful place on a bank by a river. And these two women got to the U.S., where they found peace—and my English class.

In our family, we enjoyed talking about our dreams. My father had several ones about climbing in the second-floor window of Macy's and entering the toy department. My mother once dreamed, after a visit to Africa, that she was being chased by a water buffalo. She rolled out of bed and broke her hip! I used to have recurring dreams about going back and forth over the George Washington Bridge, and cleaning a musty, dusty Victorian house, particularly a bedroom with a small, grimy window and large, dusty pillows and quilts that needed to be cleaned or thrown out; I was often in houses that belonged to someone else; those dreams stopped, and for the last eleven years, I have, for the first time in my life, owned my own home. How freeing that is!

One other important dream occurred when I first moved to Santa Barbara. I dreamed that I was wasting away, receding into nothingness. I was newly wed and working to support my then-husband so he could go to the community college to get an AA degree. I equate this dream with the painting by Michelangelo in which God is about to touch life into Adam's finger. In my dream, a human energy was about to touch me and draw me back towards life. At that time, I felt that my life was empty, because I had not yet found activities to enjoy or friends to enjoy them with, and neither Larry nor I knew very much about communicating with each other. That began to change: One day, when I was working on the switchboard of St. Francis Hospital, a good-looking Mexican man started chatting, or rather flirting, with me and feigned great surprise that I didn't have any children: "*What? No childrens?*" he queried in wonderment.

I was shocked to realize that my marriage was as desolate as the rest of my life, and I wanted to be a mother to a real child; so began the climb up the mountain of conscious change, beginning, not surprisingly, with my decision to have a child and take voice lessons. Somewhere in there, I had a dream—or imagined—that I was leading a multitude of people in a joyous song and dance in the clouds. It seems like a paradox, to have a dream with such joy when real life was so empty, but maybe not: I was having a child and starting to sing. Yes!

MY NINTH-GRADE BIBLE TEACHER taught me two interesting concepts that often show up in literature. The first is that from the deepest despair can come the greatest joy; the second, that when two things appear to be contradictory, on a higher level there is no conflict. Her major example: Scientists, who support evolution, are not heretics, for they can see and respect the wonder of the universe and life. Creationists can't get beyond dogma, or, as William Blake would say, "the mind-forged manacles." Dogma sans love is destructive, or, as Balzac would say, "Love is to the moral nature what the sun is to the earth" (two of my favorite quotes).

Blake also wrote:

> *The vision of Christ that thou dost see*
> *Is my Vision's Greatest Enemy.*
> *Thine has a great hook nose like thine,*
> *Mine has a snub nose like to mine*
> *Thine is a friend to all mankind*
> *Mine speaks in parables to the Blind.*
> *Thine loves the same world that mine hates,*
> *Thy Heaven doors are my Hell Gates.*
> *Socrates taught what Meletus*
> *Loathd as a Nation's bitterest Curse,*
> *And Caiaphas was in his own Mind*
> *A benefactor to Mankind:*
> *Both read the Bible day & night,*
> *But thou read'st black where I read white.*

Blake certainly had his own dreams. Or imaginings. Or visions. After all, there aren't too many people around who say they have dined with Joan of Arc, John the Baptist, Moses, the Angel Gabriel, and other such luminaries.

From the following story come two dreams, but they need background information:

RICHARD E. NELSON: "CHARMING, BUT UNSTABLE"

In about 1972, when I was taking voice lessons and singing a lot, I got a call from my friend Rosalie; she also studied voice with a male teacher, Richard Weiss. Rosalie had been out to Santa Barbara's Fig Tree Restaurant (named from the fact that a large fig tree stood in the center of it, inhabited by some koala bears, enclosed in glass).

Rosalie was quite excited. When she was sitting in the piano bar area, she met two men, Richard Nelson and John (Red) Fox. They told her that they were producing *A Funny Thing Happened on the Way to the Forum*. They were auditioning, and since they'd heard Rosalie singing at the piano bar, probably "Indian Love Call," they thought she would be fine for the chorus, and did she have any friends who might be interested in auditioning. Thus her call to me. She was going to the theater, the Santa Barbara Playhouse, the following Saturday, and asked me to come, too.

So I joined her inside a spacious, converted warehouse on the corner of Carrillo and Anacapa Streets. We went through the front double doors and saw no one, so we walked past the stage to the back, the shop. The shop was a large, open space directly behind the stage. Along the shop side stood a drafting desk and stool, a medium- sized office desk with a phone, two used couches, seven or eight folding chairs, and, lastly, a beat-up copy machine, the kind that needed ink and with a barrel that had to be turned manually. Farther back there was a side door, some large frames and canvas, and pots containing theatre glue, supposedly made of hooves, with its musty odor. John (Red) Fox, about 5'10", with his red-gray hair and a reddish face, a bit round in the middle, noticed us first.

"*Richard*," he called out, and nodded in our direction. Dick, slightly bald, with brown hair and mustache, and blue, blue eyes, was shirtless. There was a pause, giving them time to observe these two women who had just appeared: Rosalie, shorter than I, who had short, dark wavy hair and blue eyes, reminded me of a hummingbird when she sang; and I, whose auburn hair was long at the time and parted in the middle, and who had pierced my ears—my attempt at being a California hippie, minus the drugs and communes.

We said we'd like to audition for the show. Rehearsals had just started, so we sang for Jim Cooke, the pianist, and got copies of the script, the music, and the lowdown on the blocking. Red played Pseudalus, and a singer/actor named Gordon something played Hysterium. It was pure fun. Red was short, round, and redheaded, and Gordon tall, dark, and effeminate; this odd couple had played the same roles twice before and improvised on the script so much that it was hard not to laugh, on stage or off. There was much ado made of the gluing of jewels in the navels of the harem. The show was to open on New Year's Eve.

Red loved doing a snow job on the girls new to show biz with the line: "Stick with me, baby, and I'll show you the ropes." He and Dick liked to use the phrase "grab-assing" and emphasized the importance of the casting couch in the producer's office—in this place, the whole back space behind the stage.

Well, Rosalie and I thought, given that the show was opening on New Year's Eve and the champagne would be flowing freely after the show, we would stay around until about 11:55 p.m. and then duck out to Carrow's Restaurant a few doors down and have a congenial cup of coffee before going home and to bed. That way, we would avoid the "grab-assing" and sloppy-wet, booze-saturated kisses.

Besides, we both had kids at home who needed baby-sitting. It worked well.

So for the next six weeks there was a run-through on Wednesday night and then shows Thursday, Friday, and Saturday nights, with two Sunday matinees.

ONE WEDNESDAY NIGHT AFTER THE RUN-THROUGH, Rosalie and I went up to the Fig Tree and sang a few songs with Carol, the pianist. Dick and Red came up a little later, and we sat around the piano, sang, and chatted. There were lots of entertaining innuendoes flying around. It was laugh time. I was sitting next to Dick, who, after some chit-chat, asked if he might go home with me. There had been some talk about his ex-wife, with whom he was living. I asked him if that was so, and he said yes, it was, but it was strictly for the sake of the theater and their ten-year-old daughter Meaghan. After placing that proposition in my lap, he waited politely for my answer. I was taken aback. I hardly knew him. I thought it might be something I would *love* to do but said I didn't know him well enough. So we went to our separate homes, though I realized I was so attracted to him I could hardly see straight; I literally broke into hives!

Some time later, I learned that Dick's ex-wife, Elliott Schaffner Neuman, with whom he lived, was bipolar, and that he had given up his job in Tucson to come to Santa Barbara for the sake of his daughter; Elliott tended to drink when feeling low, and a caretaker had called Dick out of concern for the well-being of his daughter.

And they could pursue their dream of having a community theater.

The following Wednesday night, again, the four of us were at the Fig Tree. This time, Dick made an unwanted comment about my hang-ups for not going to bed with him. It didn't feel good. I was having trouble with my ingrained Victorian reserve. I had been a teenager in the era when mixed messages related to good girls: home at nine and in bed by midnight; and nice girls, in bed by nine and home by midnight. Good girls were unsexy and awkward; nice girls were sophisticated, self-assured, and worldly. I wished I could be in the latter category, but I wasn't. I felt the stigma deeply. Sexual profiling, we might call it today.

WHEN THE RUN OF *FUNNY THING* ENDED, I *had* to go back. I *had* to learn about theatre. I was shy, but I wanted to be able to perform and grab an audience. It hit me, at age thirty-one, that this was what I wanted to do. Teaching ESL was easy, since I'd had grammar all through high school and majored in French. But theater, where the mind and the body work together, that was the way it should be, and it reflected human life and emotion, and contained life lessons to enjoy and learn.

I did go back. I told Dick I wanted to do something else.

He asked me if I wanted to be in *Punch and Judy*, the children's show that Red was directing. Rehearsals had already started, so they created a non-speaking part for shy me. I was a clown and had to lead a mini-parade and beat a drum on cue. That was great, a dream fulfilled in a way. As the rehearsals continued, Dick asked me if I would do publicity for the children's shows: run off flyers

he designed and get approval from the school district office to dis-
tribute them. I had a partial connection to the schools—my six
year-old son, Anthony, was in elementary school. Dick was smart
enough to add on jobs a little at a time—very smart, because I
would have become overwhelmed if I'd known how much there
was to do.

But I was afraid of something about the theater even though I
was so drawn to it. After my morning Adult Education ESL classes
at Santa Barbara City College were over, I'd ride my bike home, get
the mail, and read it over coffee and a cigarette. Then I'd go to the
theater. But then, I'd walk around the block several times before
going inside: I remembered my mother saying many times, "Oh,
yes, we had relatives who were actors. They were very charming
. . .but *unstable*."

There was this mystery about Dick living with his ex-wife,
though not as man and wife. Elliott had no interest in sex, I learned,
but they lived together, and I was in love with him. He and Elliott
were okay with their situation, but it caused me great anxiety. He
would look at me with his blue eyes crackling and say, "Well, Natalie, yes or no?" If he'd just asked me to go for a cup of coffee and
a chat, he'd have had me in a flash, but he didn't, and I didn't have
the guts to ask him. God, how could I have been so chicken? So
much for growing up in a "nice," upper middle-class community.

One afternoon I was in the back of the theater when the phone
rang. "Santa Barbara Playhouse/Plays for Children," I answered.

"Oh, hello—is Dick there?" The woman on the line sounded
very pleasant.

"I haven't seen him yet today," I answered. "Shall I give him a message? This is Natalie."

"Oh, yes, Natalie. This is Elliott. He's mentioned you are helping with the publicity for the children's plays. Just tell him I called, and ask him to call me back."

"I will do so."

"Thank you."

I got to know Elliott, who had no reservations about saying that their purpose in being together was the sake of their daughter and the theater. That was a relief to me. And she did come to the theater occasionally, and we had some conversations at her home as well as at the theater.

ELLIOTT

Elliott Schaffner Nelson Neumann was the granddaughter of Mr. Schaffner of Hart, Schaffner, & Marx of New York and thus born into a wealthy family. Her father and her aunt were bipolar. "When my mother died, my father married Ruth, my stepmother, and she still lives in the house they bought about thirty years ago. I'm not particularly fond of her, but we can use her house and swimming pool for cast parties, as long as we clean up and don't steal anything. I came here and stayed with them after I divorced Frank Neuman. Among other things, I didn't like the way Frank treated Meaghan. Now my daughter can be with her real father, and she's very fond of him. I hope she doesn't inherit this condition. I am tired of seeing shrinks. One of them suggested that I wanted to be a boy because I preferred pants to skirts. How stupid is that? I should go horseback riding in Central Park and wear a skirt?"

Elliott was very intelligent and quite beautiful, rather short, about five feet four, with long, silky black hair framing a small, square face that sometimes looked distant but also showed that she had a sense of humor. She and Dick seemed more like sister and brother than husband and wife. Her home on a hill was comfortable, with a bookcase facing a large window that looked over Santa Barbara and the Pacific, beautiful at sunset. A large wooden dining table on one side of the living room opened into a kitchen, and opposite that area the hallway led to the bedrooms. Elliott liked to sit on the couch by the bookcase and read, or look out the large window across from her and see lower Santa Barbara and the deep blue Pacific. Who wouldn't? The aura was relaxed and comfortable. When she and Dick were living in Tucson, while Dick worked in the University's theater department, she'd raised goats, almost a hundred of them. She was also cast in numerous plays and was a fine actress. But when Meaghan was very young, she had left Dick and married a Mr. Neuman, which hadn't worked out; thus her move to Santa Barbara to her late father and step-mother. It was from her that I learned more about Dick.

DICK NELSON

Dick grew up in Altoona, Pennsylvania. His father was Welsh, his mother probably as well. He had a sister, though she wasn't mentioned at all. His father had worked in a theater in Altoona and died of pneumonia when Dick was in his teens; he'd had a bad cold but wouldn't go home until all the lights were hung in time for the opening of a show. It'd taken all night. He'd gone home with pneumonia and died in a coma within a week.

Dick then worked as the breadwinner and, some time later, joined the marines and served in the Korean War. He was shot at, which left him with pins in his lower legs, and shrapnel continued to work its way out of his body for many years after. At one time he suffered excruciating headaches; no one could detect the cause.

Finally, after spending months in the psychiatric ward of an army hospital, an x-ray showed a piece of metal at the top of his spine. It was removed; the headaches vanished, and he was discharged. He'd also contracted malaria and would occasionally have cold sweats; he did assure me that he was unable to create babies because of that virus.

When Dick was discharged from the marines, he enrolled in the theater department at Carnegie Tech, paid for by Uncle Sam. Technical theater was his bag, and he learned every aspect of it. He could make masks, posters, sets, lighting designs, and, like his father, was a competent stagehand. Elliott talked about how, when Edith Piaf performed in New York, when the curtains opened and the spotlight fell on the Little Sparrow in her black dress and her pendent in the shape of a cross, even the hardened stage hands had to wipe their eyes. And after talking to him about his earlier days in New York theater, I realized he had probably been working there when I accompanied a classmate on her thirteenth birthday to see *Guys & Dolls* with Vivian Blaine and Stubby Kaye. I later got the record of songs from that show and played them all until I knew them by heart.

Of course I learned other things about Dick and Elliott, in the course of helping with the publicity of the children's shows and later being cast in speaking parts. In *Punch and Judy* Dick was becoming dissatisfied with Red's direction; Red had had no experience in children's theater. So one Saturday morning, when Red had an appointment, Dick sat the cast down on the edge of the stage and told us that everything had to be bigger than life, that all our movements had to be more exaggerated, and that we needed more dynamics and to get our young audience to react and interact with us more. After that pep talk, we played it all bigger. I could feel the show coming to life, and we got very energetic responses from the audience, especially in the chase scenes through the audience. It was magical! Just a few suggestions and everyone came to life!

Except for Red, when he returned the next day and saw a different show. He was pissed off big time that his direction had been usurped. His red face got even redder. He swore a lot. Dick, knowing that this would happen, had made himself scarce after the show, so the cast got the heat from Red's angry venting. Dick, though, had a talent for playing games with game players: "Don't fuck with an old fucker," he liked to remind us.

DURING THE COURSE of the Santa Barbara Playhouse/Plays for Children, our copy machine started giving us problems, and we needed to buy a new one. Dick and I went up to the office supply store and found a very nice one that worked well without its ink getting all over everything. He set up a payment plan with the store's owners: something like $50.00 a month, $425.00 total, and then, nodding in my direction, said to the owner, "I taught her everything she knows." Now which movie did that line come from?

But at the end of each month, Dick didn't pay the amount due, so I had to go the store and negotiate with them. They were very patient, and I didn't blame them for getting angry. I was mortified that Dick could be so cavalier but at the same time admired his care-free audacity. I did my best to make some kind of regular payments, even if not the full amount. Later I did the same with the rent payments. And the royalties.

And the photographer—but I get ahead of myself. I was becoming involved in the business end of the theater; I was officially named the bookkeeper. I loved working in the environment, in that huge building with the front part empty and the interesting world back stage, with the glue pots, the dust, the drafting board, the copy machine, the designs Dick could draft for publicity or the set of a stage; it was an all-encompassing world in that cavernous work-place, dust and all—except that, at first, if I was working in the the-ater alone and Red came in, he always put the make on me. One day, I was standing at a desk with Audrey, a tall, lean, savvy, and classy woman and seasoned actress, who helped with the adult the-ater publicity. Red came in and put his arms around both of us. Audrey admonished, "Now, now Red, don't turn yourself on!" What a great line! My way of dealing with Red was to be at the op-posite end of the theater.

I could have made a career of working in the theater, except for the fact that no one got paid, unless an Equity actor told the pro-ducer he wouldn't report his current role to Equity and later said they'd found out and that the theater was obliged to pay.

That was tough when we couldn't pay our regular bills. The rent and the royalties and all the other expenses were next to impossible to pay. We discussed these issues a lot. We had our adult theater, children's theater, and then we started an avant-garde branch called Theater Paradox. There were many dedicated people working to make it a real community theater. With the children's plays, no child would be turned away for lack of funds. I invited all my ESL students and their children to come to the Plays for Children. Some of the plays were written by local writers, and Dick wrote a hilarious version of *Jack and the Beanstalk*:

The golden harp sings the mean green-faced giant to sleep. Jack tiptoes past the sleeping giant's chair, picks up the hen and her golden eggs and the harp and tip-toes toward the beanstalk. The giant sniffs, wakes up.

"Fee fi fo fum! . . . .I smell. . .a boy!" and the chase begins, to old-time chase music. After two minutes of this schtick, the music changes to soft, romantic dinner music. Jack places a white napkin on his arm; the giant sits down.

Jack places a full dinner plate on the table. He pours a glass of milk to go with it and the giant commences to eat. Jack gets to the bean stalk and disappears. The giant, chewing happily, says to his red-headed, loud-voiced wife, "That was a very nice boy, dear. . .boy! And the Chase resumes.

Some fine actors played at the Santa Barbara Playhouse, and I had an opportunity to play various roles and I loved it: Mrs. Cratchit in *Scrooge*, Prince Charming in *Cinderella*, with the stepmother and stepsisters in drag as in the English pantomimes; I stage managed *Reynard the Fox*; I stenciled a wallpaper pattern in *Arsenic and Old Lace*, and I made bundt cakes and lemonade for *entre-acte* refreshments. I took flyers to the elementary schools and picked up the cash box after the intermissions, which allowed me to see the last acts of each performance of the plays, each being different as each audience's reactions were different. As bookkeeper, I then joined the board of directors, and for several years I filled out the forms to be sent to the IRS. That was a chore I didn't like. Anthony was going to be in a children's play, but he didn't like it and was let off the hook, much to his relief.

I loved the theater; I was in love with the producer; I had a part-time teaching job; I worked as a parent liaison through Head Start at Anthony's school, and I became a rep for *World Book* and *Child Craft Encyclopedia*.

I had grown my hair out, too, in keeping with my own hippy self-image.

But going at that pace started to wear me down. I saw in the mirror that the edges of my mouth were turning down. I felt guilty that I didn't spend more time with Anthony, and he was giving the baby-sitter a hard time, obviously resentful of a mother who didn't have much time for him, so I felt guilty on top of being over-extended.

A BRIGHT NOTE

When I was about five months pregnant, I had learned from my relatives about a woman who taught voice, Mrs. Lura Dolas. I'd made an appointment to see her, having discovered that she'd learned piano at the age of five, attended New York's Julliard

School of Music, and been a singer herself; she was loved, appreciated, and respected by my cousin's sister-in-law, whose musically versatile daughter, a student of Mrs. Dolas, had been singing in piano bars and church choirs at the time.

Mrs. Dolas lived on Crestline Drive in Santa Barbara, on an elevated ridge, allowing a viewer to see the green-brown hills on one side of the city, and Shoreline Drive and the ocean on the other. She was a short, buxom woman with thick, brown, wavy hair parted in the middle and tied in a bun, and she had a kind yet focused demeanor. I felt trust and respect for her as soon as we started talking.

"First," she advised, "wait until your baby is born before starting the lessons, because carrying him will have an effect on your breathing. Second, it's not likely that you will be able to have a career starting at this time in your life." (That was no problem for me; I just wanted to learn to sing well despite my shyness and a voice placed too far back in my throat, as if I were hiding.) "Usually," she added, "it takes about five years for one to make a smooth bridge between their high register and their low register."

Her rates were very reasonable: $20.00 an hour. (This was in 1967.) Mrs. Dolas also worked in the musical productions of Santa Barbara Junior High and Santa Barbara High, and was a member of the Santa Barbara Woman's Club, which sometimes asked for her students to come and give an afternoon's entertainment. So I had something to look forward to once Anthony was born, and I could bring him with me to the lessons!

March 27, 1967, the day after Easter and two weeks early, Anthony Francis Califano, named by his father, Lawrence Francis Califano, joined us here on Earth, and my mother came from Engle-wood, New Jersey to welcome him. Labor time: three hours—not bad for a first baby! What an indescribable feeling, when he was cleaned, wrapped, and given to me to hold and look into his eyes looking into mine. Now I was ready to sing!

I got myself a cheap child's keyboard and started singing scales. It sounded so bad I would cry! Anthony was happily on a blanket on the floor during my lessons, and we could watch him, fascinated to notice his evolving changes, all the involuntary funny smiles and grimaces, to real smiles and laughter. Larry too laughed when watching all his faces. And how first he lifted his head, then his crawling, then balancing on two arms and one leg, and then walking, though by then I had a baby-sitter since I was back at work on a part-time basis.

MY FIRST RECITAL

Mrs. Dolas, being from the old school, believed that singers of classical music should learn to project sans microphone, and to build my voice and my breathing power, she started me on Handel: "Where E'er You Walk," "He Shall Feed His Flock," "O Thou that Tellest Good Tidings to Zion," and "For Unto Us a Child Is Born," which I especially loved for obvious reasons, and then French and Italian art songs and *leider*. So when it came time for me to sing in front of an audience, Mrs. Dolas chose "Me Voici Dans Son Boudoire" (Here I Am In Her Boudoir!), usually sung by a mezzo, a woman playing the part of a young man. It was held at the Woman's Club in Santa Barbara. As I walked down the center aisle, my right knee was shaking so badly that I thought I would fall down, and the right edge of my mouth was twitching. But I got through the song.

The audience was made up of family and friends of the students, and one of the most promising of her students was Ed Cook, who was in many of his school productions and whose family, including his aunt and uncle, came. His uncle, Dick Galway, came up to me and told me he enjoyed my singing. It was several years later, after he and his son, Richard, had taken some lessons from Mrs. Dolas and another teacher, that I was to come across him again, and we remembered that first meeting.

A Son and a Divorce

The first two years of Anthony's life were joyful ones, even though Larry and I weren't on the same page. We both laughed at Anthony's involuntary face-making stage, and Larry learned to change diapers and didn't always go out to play pool every night as he had before March 27, 1967. He did some work making our run-down kitchen a bit nicer with the help of a neighbor, Dick, who was good at fixing up houses, and we occasionally had dinner with him and his wife, Mary. Mary was partially blind but a wonderful cook; Dick was good-natured but seriously opinionated. They had both become Mormons and thus avoided all caffeine and alcohol. They lived on the same property as we did, in the small, two-floor house with brown siding across the driveway and closer to the street, where Lydia and Mike had lived earlier. Our little run-down house in the back was connected to the garages at the end of the property and lay behind the house with four apartments in front.

We had moved into one of *those* four apartments at first, for $75.00 a month, and when the opportunity came to move to the house in back, we'd kept the same rent for quite a few years.

Another neighbor, Bess, who referred to Dick and Mary as "Yo-yo" and "Wonder Girl," lived in one of the front apartments; her philosophy was that you should try everything once. One day she came over and said to me, "Natalie, I'm getting married, and I'm having the reception in *your* house." Bess Carhardt had grown up in a wealthy family in New York City but come to California to find something different and to get away from family and lifestyle. She had met a young Mexican-American man, and there had been im-mediate chemistry, though it had worn off shortly thereafter. Bess had fair skin and a petite, heart-shaped face with wavy, light brown hair, and, as she was losing weight, the heart-shaped face and her gray-green eyes became more prominent.

And so, one Saturday, I went to work from 7:30 a.m. to 3:00 p.m., came home, and readied the place for this event, putting Anthony in his crib for a nap. Bess was a great cook and hostess; the refreshments served were wonderful; it was a mixed and good crowd, Jack's family and friends as well as some of Bess's. We en-joyed a mix of Mexican and pop music. The occasion was a success, although I had a splitting headache and Anthony was in discomfort due to gas; fortunately, one of one of Bess's friends, a nurse, took him in hand while Larry and I hosted. When all the guests had left, I went upstairs to relax with Anthony. On my bed, I ran my fingers around his eyebrows and lips and watched him make funny faces when softly tickled. Then I felt drowsy, and the pain in my head dissipated. I drifted into a sweet sleep with my baby next to me, this little cherub with curly blond hair and blue eyes. It was bit of peace after a hectic week.

About a month after the wedding, Bess came over. She had circles under her eyes and looked pale and drained. She and Jack had had numerous differences and had split. She'd had a conversation with Jack's mother, who'd basically told her that men could have women and shake themselves off and go on from there, but that, when women were with men, they were tainted from then on. And, given the break-up, Bess had opted to have an abortion.

However, life changed for her sometime later.

When Anthony was first born, I had taken six weeks off from work in the business office of St. Francis Hospital and then gone back part-time, leaving Anthony with my cousin by marriage, Pam, who had two small children of her own. But Larry and I didn't really communicate, and I felt that I was doing it all—housework, cooking, and mostly mothering. I had suggested a separation at some point, but he wasn't amenable to that, so I'd simply waited, both of us living in something of a vacuum.

FRANKIE

What changed that was Larry's brother, Frank, coming to visit on his way back from Viet Nam. It was fun to have him, and he and Larry were close and funny together, laughing about some of the TV programs they enjoyed as kids, such as *The Honeymooners* and *The Three Stooges*: "Hello! Ya don't say. . .ya don't say. . . ya don't say. . .ya don't say," etc. "Who was that?" "He didn't say."

Frank went to New York for close to a year, but he came back to Santa Barbara, found an apartment on Euclid Avenue, around the corner from us and between us and Highway 101, and enrolled at Santa Barbara City College, having, as his brother had, taken the initial placement test, and then continued to complete his AA degree.

These two brothers, born in St. Luke's Hospital in 1940 and 1943, looked like brothers, with their thick black hair and clear blue eyes under prominent foreheads, tall, slender builds, and New York accents. They helped each other during periods of adversity in their lives, starting with their dropping out of Rice Catholic School, which had been run by the tough Christian Brothers. Later, they faced some kind of breakdown of their mother, Molly Sweeney Califano, the oldest of about eighteen children in Ireland, who had only had about four years of schooling in the old country. During the eight-year period of her breakdown, the boys had lived with their father, Ralph, and their Uncle Otto—a period of calm.

One night, Larry and I sat down, and he told me he would move in with his brother and acknowledged that it wasn't right to stay together with so little communication. He didn't take much, just his clothes and personal belongings. I felt relief, not just that he was moving out, but more importantly, that he had spoken honestly and acknowledged the situation for what it was.

SOMEWHERE ABOUT THAT TIME, I got a call from Bess, who had moved out of 410 West Sola Street and had been in New York City for a while. "Natalie," she announced, "a whole new world has opened up for me!"

"What's that?" I asked.

"The gay world, the gay world," she exulted.

"Oh, that's good," I said. "If it's right for you, then it's a good thing."

Some weeks later, I heard a knock at my door about 8:00 p.m. There was Bess, wearing a long blue velour caftan with a matching band in her hair. She looked a lot better than the last time I had seen her, post-abortion. "Natalie, I'm very happy. I'm engaged! Would you like to meet her? She's in the car!"

"Of course, bring her in." And in came Judy, a physical education teacher at Santa Barbara High School. We chatted over a glass of wine.

"I bought a nice house on the top of Milpas Street, by Santa Barbara High School," Bess told me, "and we will have you over for dinner soon. How's little Ignats?" (her name for Anthony).

"Oh, he's fine. I have a good babysitter right next to the hospital, for only fifty cents an hour, and she's approved by the Department of Welfare and tells me all the things he's learning, I didn't know he liked ketchup, and I can pick him up on my bike and carry him home in a baby backpack. And in the morning, I wake up and listen to him talk to himself with sounds, not words, and it cracks me up. He's asleep now, but you can take a peek at him if you like."

They took a quick look and went off to their nice new home.

I did go there for dinner a few weeks later and, before Judy came home from work, asked Bess how married life was.

"It's just like being married to a man. Judy goes to work early in the morning, and I do the cooking and cleaning, and when she gets home, she puts on her slippers and reads the paper. Then I serve dinner, and she watches TV and naps while I do the dishes."

"...Well, the house definitely has your imprint in it. I'm looking at those gorgeous yellow-orange flowered curtains, how they match the deeper orange rug and couch, and some of your blown glass ornaments. It looks and feels comfortable, and you *are* probably one of the best cooks in Santa Barbara."

"I do love to cook. And Natalie, I still say, you should try everything at least once." I thought I knew what she was referring to, but it wasn't for me. I asked myself seriously on numerous occasions if it might be, but no, it just didn't grab me, if you get my drift.

Judy got home, and we had a lovely dinner that included broccoli with Hollandaise and roast lamb, mashed potatoes and salad, and Pepperidge Farm rolls.

I didn't see much of Bess after that, as our activities didn't coincide, but her presence in my life came during those years when I had to make some difficult decisions for myself, and she had been most generous when Anthony was born, buying many things for him and sharing in my joy. I'll always picture her in the blue velour caftan and matching headband, as well as in her short dresses and tall boots—a *fashionista* ahead of her time.

I was still working at St. Francis part time, and I did get called to fill in for a few hours if needed. On occasion, if I couldn't get a baby sitter, I would bring Anthony in with me—a little hectic when feeding a baby in the small, square admitting office while the phone was ringing or someone came in to register for admission.

One evening, José, one of the housekeeping staff, came into my office and sat across from me. "I have to be admitted," he said very seriously. He had a hardy build and short, curly hair with traces of gray—a good-looking Mexican with the shiny white teeth of a man who had never needed a dentist. He rather reeked of sexuality.

"What's the diagnosis?" I asked, taking out an admission form and putting it in the typewriter.

"*Dolor*," he said, which means "pain."

"*Dolor?*" I asked.

"*Dolor de corazon.*" (That means "heartache.")

I pursed my lips. José had told me well over a year before, before I was pregnant, that he wasn't happy in his marriage, and that he wanted me. I had told him that adultery was a cause for divorce, and at a later time that he was more Mexican than Catholic. And, of course, the Victorian fingers in my mind were pointing emphatically as I contemplated telling my parents I was having an affair with a man who spoke little English, hadn't finished junior high school, and had no problem with having women on the side, "unhappily married" or not.

Ironically, St. Francis Hospital, although Catholic, had closed down its maternity ward and replaced it with an eye clinic, causing me to have Anthony at Cottage Hospital. But when Anthony was only nine months old, at the St. Francis Hospital Christmas party, Anthony, José, and I were in a tableau depicting the Holy Family, while Dr. Larry Williams played "Silent Night" on his guitar and Anthony made singing noises behind the curtains to accompany him!

José had also brought me a potted chrysanthemum as a congratulatory gift for having Anthony. I was grateful, because in my mind he had (figuratively) planted the seed when he acted so shocked after I said I had no children; it had made me realize with a shock how much I wanted a child. It had thus been an immaculate conception of sorts.

Anthony's first word was "hi!"—not a surprise, since I said that to him every morning. When he was a little older and I took him out in his stroller, he would put out his left hand to every passerby and say, "Hi!"

But during the first two years of Anthony's life, Larry and I weren't communicating much better than we had before I got pregnant. He *had* learned to change diapers, but he didn't help around the house and still went out to play pool. People noticed it, and some friends mentioned to me that they could see something wasn't right with our marriage.

We had Anthony baptized in the Presbyterian Church, but we didn't attend much. The young couples our age were decent, affluent, upper middle-class people and had a lifestyle different from ours. I was not comfortable with them, coming from a lower-income family, my father being an unconventional, free-thinking, low-paid private boys school teacher and atheist, and my mother a working woman. Larry couldn't relate to these couples at all, having grown up in a somewhat seedy neighborhood in New York, having started working at fourteen while his mother took all the money he earned, and many of his old buddies were in and out of jail, though his best friend, Eddie Hopkins, cared about him enough to tell him, when he was beginning to play around with drugs, to get out and join the marines.

I didn't really have a desire to attend church every Sunday, as there were so many other things to do on a Sunday morning: play with Anthony, take a walk, have friends over, or stay home and clean and/or read the paper. But I rarely spent Sunday morning with Larry. Once when we were walking down State Street *together*, I was feeling light-hearted, and Larry, noticing it, asked rather cynically, "What are you so happy about?"

"Because the three of us are doing something together," I explained. He had reason to have some resentment towards me, though, and took it out by letting me do everything in the house.

When Larry did move around the corner with Frankie, I stayed up late that first night reading Leon Uris's *Exodus*, feeling relaxed and relieved enough in the new space. Having taken Spanish at Adult Education for two years, it occurred to me that I might be able to teach English in the City College Adult Education Program. One sunny afternoon in June, I stopped by the Adult Ed office on my way home and asked if I could teach an ESL night class.

"Just fill out this application," answered a pleasant secretary. "That's all," she cheerfully added. "And then you can speak with the ESL Coordinator, Paul Ash." It was true that I had taken two other languages and would know more English than the students I would have, but I was shocked that I didn't need any other training!

Paul Ash, a tall, slender, sandy-haired man, came out of his office right then, and we made an appointment. He told me that, if any kind of workshops or conferences came up, he would contact me, and, in fact, I was able to attend a five-day conference at a hotel in San Diego, which was very useful.

It was also the first time I had taken the time to do such a thing in many years. I roomed with a woman twenty years older than I and met many likeable teachers, including a group of Mexican-Americans teaching from elementary level to adult level in Arizona. They sensed that I was having a difficult time, being recently separated, and I enjoyed their warmth and humor.

One Adult Ed teacher used to knock on doors in his neighborhood and beyond to recruit students to come to class, stressing the importance of learning the language. Another one of the presenters would tap out the rhythm of American phrasing with a pencil, or clap, and have the students repeat it.

One of the teachers, Arthur Arvizu (the name is Basque, but for all practical purposes he was Mexican-American), and I had an instant rapport. Walking to one of the sessions, he said to me, "You Americans have no culture."

"Come to my father's house," I said, "and you will change your mind." But he was a committed teacher, not to mention good for my ego—and nice looking: short, with a square face, thick, wavy salt-and-pepper hair, and he loved people. He lived in Los Angeles with a pretty wife and four children. I came close to spending the last night with him, but logistics are dicey in these situations, and the Victorian fingers were pointing at me in any case.

Back in Santa Barbara, life went on as it had before I left.

On one occasion, José drove me home from work, but before then wanted to stop by his two-bedroom Spanish-style house to pick up something. I came in with him, feeling very guilty. The house was all on one level, the front door opening from a small porch into the living room; the master bedroom was on one side, the kitchen straight ahead. As he picked up something on the kitchen table and we walked towards the door, he suddenly grabbed me, threw me on his bed, and quickly unbuckled his belt, opened his fly, and dropped his khaki pants revealing his white choners (an nickname for men's underwear) and his muscular abdomen, but was too rushed to perform, and I was quite frantic, wondering if Maria might come in the door any minute, though later he explained that he was going to pick her up. As we walked out his front door and onto his porch and a beautiful sunny day, I realized with great relief that nothing had changed; the beautiful, sunny sky hadn't fallen because of it. I was truly amazed! There was no scarlet letter on either of our chests!

We had one other attempt in the back of his car some time later, when, after work on a sunny day, he drove me to a beach in Hope Ranch and we made an attempt in the back seat of his car. But there was no leg room, no elbow room, and no leverage. I had never practiced messing around in the back seat of a car—though I can't speak for him in that respect.

I felt very uncomfortable being in that situation, and he would sometimes seem to be happy, without a care in the world, and at others very sad. I wondered what was going on with him and knew that I would need to tell Larry one day why it had happened.

AFTER ABOUT TWO YEARS OF THIS continuing undercurrent of sexual tension and anxiety, I found an opportunity to have José come over when Larry was away visiting his buddy John Flaherty, who had moved to Los Angeles in order to put himself through college and study acting.

I told José I would be home alone one Friday night. He duly came over; I was nervous; it was probably five or so in the afternoon. Without much ado, we went into the kitchen, where he tried to have sex on the rickety kitchen table. That didn't work, so he left, laughing.

When all else fails, laugh! I laughed and laughed. All that angst, tension, frustration, secrecy, and sadness ended with a laugh. But I was tired of the secrecy and the lack of communication all around, so I made a plan to meet José's wife, Maria. Their two children, Teresa and Lourdes (Teré and Lulu) went to a Head Start preschool. I went there and offered to volunteer.

The director, Josie Schrier, was happy to have me, so I went the morning I worked late at St. Francis Hospital. I met the two precious girls along with all the other children and saw how they were all preparing for kindergarten, learning the alphabet and writing their names along with songs and games. As I chatted with Josie, I learned that José's wife, Maria, was unhappy with her marriage, and Josie said she needed someone to talk to because she wanted to start divorce proceedings and was very stressed, and that Josie herself was probably the only other adult whom she had confided in.

I met Maria one day at a little party at the preschool. She was a beautiful woman, with classic Spanish/Indian features: long black hair, straight brows over black eyes, a squarish face and chin, a straight nose, and a full, beautiful mouth. She was about five feet four and large-boned but slender. She was also articulate and poised. I invited her to come over for coffee the following week. I told her I worked at the hospital and knew José, and practiced

Spanish with him and his co-workers, leaving the opening for her to talk, and talk she did.

"I am not happy with this man, and I don't understand him at all. When I am mean to him, he gets very sorrowful and sleeps in the car, but when I am nice to him, he is happy and then goes out looking for other women. It makes me crazy. When I was little, my father was mean to me and put me to work cleaning people's homes, but one time when I was in my teens, he took me to my two aunts' home on his horse and started getting aroused when I was sitting in front of him. I had to live with my aunts, who were mean and so religious they wouldn't let me go out at all, so to get out of that I married José, and we came here. Now we are here with two children, and this man is crazy. One time the girls were sitting on his lap and he was angry with something and stood up suddenly, just letting them fall on the floor. I went to a lawyer, who speaks Spanish, but he said I would need a witness to testify that he'd done something."

Maria had gone to see a lawyer, a kindly, older man who was bilingual. He told her she would need a witness who could testify to adultery or mental cruelty. Unsurprisingly, she felt sickened and angry when I told her we had made the effort, and I felt sick myself, and dirty, having to tell her this and seeing her reaction. The truth hurt. We parted company, she having a witness if she wanted one. I would accept, as I contemplated that I would be the logical witness.

Two days later we met again, still having the same feelings, but she asked, and I obliged. There is no satisfaction being on either end of the stick: of being the betrayed or the accomplice to the betrayal. Having been on both, I prefer to be the on the accomplice end, even though that too is sickening.

I made an appointment to see Mr. Velez, the lawyer, and when I told him we had attempted to have sex in the back seat of a car, he smiled and commented, "Sometimes we find ourselves in very strange situations. Well, Maria now has her witness."

And so, on the appointed day, a sunny Thursday afternoon two weeks later, I went to Room 16 of the elegant, Spanish-style Santa Barbara Courthouse, where I met Maria, Mr. Velez, the judge, and a transcriber. Maria, serious but poised, made her plea for divorce based on adultery, and I took the witness stand, very nervous, embarrassed, but relieved that José wasn't present. I might have passed out if he'd had come; my knees were shaky already. When asked if I had had sexual relations with José, I affirmed that I had. The judge then said, "And you did this knowing that you would be causing pain?"

I replied, with very flushed cheeks, "Yes—I've been worried about this for two years." I doubted it made an impression on anyone there, but it was true. Maria, although angry and hurt, was relieved and thanked me for helping her.

When I went back to the preschool, however, Josie Schrier was very cold to me, and it was difficult to stay in that situation, although Maria did tell me later that Josie appreciated the fact that I had done this for her. After they had their year-end graduation, I didn't go back, though I enjoyed seeing Teré—her long, straight hair and her mother's serious demeanor, and Lulu, with her father's curly hair and her more bubbly personality.

I did get to know them more later, though, after about a year.

Maria and I became friends and went out sometimes. She eventually met a decent, educated American, and I sang the "Lord's Prayer" at their wedding.

Of course, there was no conversation between José, his friends, and me when I was at the switchboard or on breaks at the hospital.

Some months passed, I continued to feel ugly and dirty, and I wished I could have gotten to know Maria under different circumstances, as she was not only beautiful but charming, intelligent, and superstitious all at the same time. Anyway, at one point that year, while I was on the switchboard, José walked by and out the door in the middle of the afternoon, jacket in hand. He looked resentful—mouth straight and eyes angry. I later learned that he had been fired on the spot, for trying to have sex with a co-worker in a broom closet.

I HAVE COME A LONG WAY from my original discussion of dreams and visions, and I have narrated backwards! I was no longer naive or frustrated because of feeling sheltered and inexperienced. That's the good news—though I travelled through some bad news situations before getting there! As for the two dreams I promised to tell, they will appear in later stories. This particular narrative has come to an end, but it is only the end of this story, which is the end of the beginning.

Desperation

Why was I so depressed and bored with life?
I didn't really know, except that,
in supporting a man still a child
and enjoying nothing,
one dull day followed another like poison
that follows the blood stream to the brain.

Then one day I saw a face:
this man's expression,
reflecting my own numb anguish,
shocked me—shocked me!

I saw his face again; this time it was different.
He was chatting and joking with his friends on a break.
Noticing me, he stopped talking
and his face became still, but looked angry.
After a moment, his mouth formed into a suave smile.

"Buenos dias, senorita!" he oozed, laying on the charm.

In the following months I saw him often at work,
sometimes laughing gaily with his friends
appearing to be without a care in the world.

At other times he looked so sad I wanted to cry,
and sometimes did—for him, for me,
for my lost husband—who can tell?

At other times I could not cry,
because the only way to save my slowly dying spirit
was to laugh—to imitate,
no matter how untrue it might have seemed,
this man, who, like myself,
was desperately afraid to die before he'd lived.

SISTER SYLVIANNE

S HORTLY AFTER I BEGAN WORKING in the business office of St. Francis Hospital, Sister Sylvianne came from the Mother House in Illinois to be the new administrator. One reason, we heard, was that she was good at putting things in order, and apparently there was a need for that, although I was new enough that I hadn't noticed. She frequently used the phrase, "ship-shape," which gave us a clear indication of what was needed in every aspect of the hospital, especially the business office.

Sister, as we called her, was fairly tall, and her face looked oval, though the wimple covering her head added to that impression. She wore the full-length black habit with a loose belt around her waist from which hung her crucifix and rosary beads, which jingled as she walked along in her black, laced boots, so we always knew when she was coming. Her face was very white; apparently she didn't sunbathe in sunny California.

For some reason, Sister seemed to harp on me. "Uh, Natalie, haven't you finished filing yet?" she asked with a look of displeasure on her face.

"No, I just came back from relieving Arthur on the switchboard." Or she would look me up and down, the way some men deliberately size up women, and say, "Uh, Natalie, are you wearing stockings?" She thought all women working there should wear stockings. Or she would tell me things about the office I already knew, until I began saying in a bored voice, "I know."

I did enjoy one game with her. As she paused at the threshold to talk to the switchboard operator, while opening the door to the business office, I would say in a loud stage whisper, "Here comes Sister!" After a month or two of her nagging, she asked me how long I had been working there.

When I told her it had been three months, she seemed surprised and said she thought I had been there much longer. In short, she thought I was slow. In the meantime, I decided that I would show *her*, and learn every aspect of the office routines, and make myself indispensable. I could work in the Admissions Office, balance the money, man the switchboard, take in payments, explain bills in Spanish, and of course, file. Sometimes accounts were misfiled. When the all-woman office personnel made a drama out of *"Who misfiled the Johnson account?"* I would say, whether it was true or not, "I have no shame. I did."

On occasion, one woman would have a spat with another. My philosophy: Offices should never be made up solely of women. (My attitude on that has changed over the years.) In any case, I was asked, when the administrative secretary was out, or sick, to cover in that office, and was flattered to be asked. Sister had acquired more respect for me. The downside of making myself indispensable was that sometimes I was asked to work on my days off, and on a few occasions called the morning of the same day they wanted me. I was not happy about that.

JOSÉ

When I worked on the switchboard in the morning, the men on the housekeeping staff were usually cleaning the floors around the front door and the long counter by the switchboard area.

One of them would always say, "Good morning," and one day he stood in front of me and stretched out both of his fists.

He said, "Choose." I picked one. He opened it and handed me a mini Tootsie Roll. That was José Sotelo, from Colima, Mexico— brown eyes, curly black hair, solidly built, about five foot eight. The features of his face were chiseled as if sculpted in rock, like his body. He knew a little English and was studying it in the Adult Education program; in José and his coworkers, I found people with whom I could practice my Spanish. One of the office girls, Anne, from the mid-West, quite small and sheltered, was afraid of Mexicans. She asked me if all of them carried knives. I asked José, "Anne wants to know if all Mexicans carry knives."

He looked surprised. "Only to clean my nails," he replied.

He once asked me, "How many childrens you have?"

"I don't have any."

He looked shocked, "*Whaaat?* You no have no *childrens?*"

"No," I said, wondering why he was acting so surprised.

Well, I did know that José was flirting with me, and it was fun to have a good-looking guy from another country do so while we practiced our respective new languages. And it offered me a bit of suggestive levity.

But recognition hit me like a sledgehammer. I wanted a child, very badly. I was twenty-six and was working so Larry could get his A.A. degree. But I wasn't doing much else; I hadn't looked for, or found, other things that I enjoyed—not Larry's problem—but also, he would come home from City College and do some home-work and then, after dinner, go out to play pool. If there was an afternoon when he didn't have class, he would go to the beautiful Spanish-style Santa Barbara Courthouse, with its sunken gardens, and sit in on some of the court hearings, fantasizing that he would become another Melvin Belli (a high-profile lawyer in the 1960s). I felt as if I were carrying the load for both of us and he wasn't there.

During this period, we had two interesting visitors. The first was Eddie Hogan, who lived above Larry's parents' apartment at 102 West 109th. We got a call from him; it seemed he had been in some kind of serious trouble and needed to get out of the city. He flew to Los Angeles, took a bus to Santa Barbara, and one day ap-peared at our door. I never did learn what he had done, but while there, he did what he did best: impersonate everyone Larry knew from his neighborhood and catch us up on what everyone was doing. His adopted dad, Johnny Hogan, had cancer; his mother, Wanda, still got up at 4:00 p.m. and went to bed at 4:00 a.m.; and Larry's father, Ralph, was still as sick and as depressed as he had been when we got married. Thomas Watters, their junkie friend, was in jail again. Eddie Hopkins, Larry's best friend, who had told Larry ten years prior to get out of the neighborhood before he got addicted to drugs, was raising his family in Hazlet, New Jersey. And Larry's younger brother, Frank, was considering enlisting.

Eddie, wild-eyed, came in in a whirlwind, entertained us, and left. If Larry knew what kind of trouble Eddie was in, he didn't tell me, though there was a hint, true or not, that he had gotten in a fight and killed someone. Eddie was smart and gifted; he had also been Larry's best man at our wedding when all Larry's other friends declined, being Catholics. Larry's mother was sad it wasn't a Catholic wedding, and his father, at the time, was in the psychiatric ward at St. Luke's Hospital, where we went after the wedding on our way to our honeymoon at the New York Hilton's bridal suite before proceeding to Woodstock, New York, the next morning.

One day, José offered to drive me home after work. I accepted. He drove me to the four hundred block of Sola Street and then stopped just around the corner. He looked serious. He said, *"Yo te quiero."*

I didn't get it at first, but when I did, I was taken aback, having learned that adultery meant divorce. I mentioned this in my new Spanish: *"Esto es el major razón por divorce!"* (grateful that so many English words had cognates in other Romance languages). I asked him why; "I am not happy," he said. He had two children, Tere (Teresa) and Lulu (Lourdes), he told me. I envied him.

It was sunny outside, but as I left José, I understood now why he sometimes looked so sad; Larry and I weren't communicating, and I felt like a person living outside life.

A few months earlier, I had dreamed that I was slowly fading, dwindling into nothingness, until a warm finger on a warm hand touched my finger and began to draw me back to life and energy. And with this realization and dream, I felt that everything about my life was all wrong.

The next day was my day off, and I proceeded to fall apart. I sat in the bathtub and cried hysterically. I then went up to our roof and lay in the sun, letting its warmth soothe me while I rested. I said to myself, "I have to take one day at a time. I have to have a baby." Larry and I needed to have something happy to give us the strength to break up, which I knew was inevitable. How I could be so attracted to one man while being married to another was another shocking realization. Larry and I hadn't had any sex for a long time, and he wasn't initiating it—not surprising, since he wasn't spending any time with me.

So one night, I initiated it; then he went to sleep, and I lay awake, crying to myself. As for José, he knew I was attracted to him and so continued to flirt with me.

HAWAII

My sister, Carol, and her husband Craig, had three children: Betsy, age seven; Stephen, five; and Charles, one and a half.

With three small children at home, they had not had any time off to themselves in a while and were feeling stressed. Our mother suggested that they go to Kauai for a break of a week or so, and that she would cover the cost of Larry and me staying with their kids. What an opportunity it was for Larry and me, as well as for Carol and Craig. And so we did, though not before I had some lab tests to see if I was pregnant. I was told to call the St. Francis lab in a week.

It was a hot August and seriously humid in Kailua, Hawaii. I was feeling quite tired but for some reason had lost my taste for coffee. Charles would notice something new and let out a happy shriek. He was a plump little thing and found a lot of things to shriek about when we took them to a drive-in theater.

Betsy, even then, was charming and pretty, with her thick dark hair and brown eyes, learning how to read and play the piano.

Stephen reminded me of my brother in looks and behavior; he was his own person and had his own ideas. He would cross his arms and be adamant about something or other, and I thought at the time that I wouldn't want to get into an argument with him any more than I would with my brother. He, with his brown hair and-blue eyes, could shimmy up a palm tree and cut off coconuts with a small machete. Stephen also introduced Larry and me to dried, salted plums and dried shrimp and scallops, which I hungrily devoured and then felt too full and nauseous. I often felt ravenous and then nauseous.

I called the lab several times but was told that only the doctor could tell me the results of the tests. In the meantime, they kept asking me if I had been eating watermelon seeds in Hawaii. I didn't get the hints! But the trip was good for everyone, and I learned to change diapers, thanks to plump, shrieking Charles. We could walk barefoot almost anyplace and often took our three wards to the beach, which was only a few blocks away.

When we returned to Santa Barbara, I called the doctor, a kind man who was also the obstetrician for my cousins, and learned the good news after being ribbed for being so dense.

Although I dragged myself to work every day for the first three months, I was happy. My name at work became *"Mamacita,"* and my co-workers kept reminding me that my time would not be my own once the baby arrived. Even Larry seemed happier; his steps were quicker when coming in the front door (there was no back door, just two windows!).

In the meantime, brother Frank did enlist and would be passing through after his training, on the way to Viet Nam.

SEPTEMBER, 1966

Frankie arrived, and the two brothers had a good time together going through their imitations of *The Three Stooges*, *The Honeymooners*, and catching up on all the characters from their neighborhood: John Tyndale, the "North of Ireland Presbyterian" who invited Larry to his "office," the doorway of any apartment building he was near, and their mother Molly's best friend, Mae Sugrue, who once mooned someone she didn't like by her front stoop; Thomas Watters, who once stole his mother's brand-new washing machine for drugs; and numerous others who hung out at Murphy's or Fell's bar on and around the corner of Amsterdam and 109th. Here were two guys in their twenties meeting in a brand-new place for perhaps the first time away from the old run-down neighborhood. It was good. I always liked Frankie, though I wouldn't have liked it if I asked where my son was going all dressed up, shaved and lotioned, and he replied, "Out."

On March, 27, 1967, the day after Easter, Anthony Francis Califano arrived and my mother came from Englewood to welcome her new and fourth grandchild into the world.

DECEMBER, 1967

After six or eight weeks of being home full-time, I went back to work three mornings a week, and my cousin, Pam, who had one son and another on the way, watched Anthony at their house in Carpenteria. As soon as I came in to pick him up, I had to go straight inside and look at him, my baby. Pam loved being a mother and gave me many tips on subjects such as dealing with diaper rash, soaking the cotton diapers (no Pampers), and heating up baby food. Larry and I were highly entertained by the involuntary expressions Anthony could show on his face, and Larry did learn to change diapers. Since I had walked to and from work for most of my pregnancy, I actually lost five pounds during that time, and after delivery, my stomach was flatter than it had been at any other time in my life.

I was still called *"Mamacita"* at work. José brought me a pink chrysanthemum plant, which I later planted and watched blossom twice a year. I planned to visit Englewood in December, after the Christmas party at St. Francis. That year they decided to have a series of tableaux. Anthony, at nine months, was a blonde, curly-haired, blue-eyed, adorable child, and I was asked to be the Virgin Mary, with Anthony as the Christ child.

And the perfect Joseph? José, of course. While we waited, in Biblical garb, Dr. Larry Williams played and sang Christmas songs on his guitar, while on stage, as yet unseen, came sounds from Anthony trying to sing with the doctor. The older I get, the more precious these moments become.

And then, we were off to New Jersey for a visit. My parents were well, but not so for Molly and Ralph at 102 West 109th. I took a bus into the city, with Anthony, on a rainy night. My mother was concerned and thought about coming to protect me. The idea *was* a bit foolhardy, though the sentiment was there; I had no concerns about going there. Anthony was crawling, and everywhere he went was something to experience without filters. I carried him up the four flights of stairs and was once again at the apartment my husband had grown up in. Ralph was in bed, Molly sitting at the kitchen table. Anthony had no concerns with the dust on the floor and he didn't have allergies, thank goodness. I don't remember much about the visit, except that at one point, Ralph said he was thirsty, to which Molly admonished, "Don't go botherin' Natalie to bring ye anything ye don't need! She has enough to do with the baby." I don't remember what I did then, but the memory has saddened me ever since. She didn't know how to care for a sick husband any more than she did her children, though she was a good cook. Larry had gone into the city earlier to see parents and friends, and went back to Santa Barbara before me.

Back in Santa Barbara, and back at St. Francis Hospital, has been described in other chapters; Larry and I separated and then divorced. I helped Maria Sotelo with her divorce from José, and later met a French professor eighteen years my senior who taught at the University of California, Santa Barbara. I was getting restless working in the business office, and some of my co-workers noticed it and said, "Natalie, you should go back to school. You need more intellectual stimulation." And, "Natalie, how is your French professor doing?" It seemed as if I was stepping into a different world. As was Larry, who had become enamored with an older woman who was a dancer. The problem with that, though, was that her ex-boyfriend was still in the picture and seemed to be driven to take revenge on Larry. Larry would come by at times, usually wearing dark glasses, and exclaim, "This is bad. It's so bad!"

Larry was then working for the Santa Barbara Department of Welfare and was good at what he did. He also had good looks and charm, and as he later told me, he needed this kind of attention because of a terrible incident when he was young in New York. A crazy, sadistic man grabbed him, took him into the basement of a building, and put the end of a lit cigarette on different parts of his body. He was afraid to tell his mother because she would blame him. Both of us, several years later, joined support groups.

But when I remember the times when I wanted to separate and Larry suggested going to a counselor, I remarked, "You can go if you want to, but I don't want to." Hindsight was better than foresight in that case.

After I left working at St. Francis and went to graduate school, got over-involved in the theater, and underwent severe stress, I met Sister Sylvianne again when I was being discharged as a patient with colitis, rheumatoid arthritis, and severe anemia. I'd had to have four pints of blood. My ankles were very swollen, and my knees ached. I was about to be wheeled onto the elevator, and as the door opened, Sister Sylvianne stepped off, and we exchanged greetings. She seemed to be more interested in looking at my legs and feet than at my face. I can only hope she understood why I wasn't wearing stockings.

Abortion (Since
The Subject Was Raised)

WHAT MAKES ME SEE RED is when some people think that they have the exclusive knowledge of God's thoughts and judgment. Take abortion, for example.

Take the people who parade in front of the library where children go to read. The pro-lifers hold up grotesque signs of bleeding fetuses warped by coat hangers, or they piously pray at the door of the abortion clinic across the street from the library. These people, with all their pious, self-righteous prayers, think that the women entering the abortion clinic have no soul or relationship with God and have no misgivings about what they feel they must do—that they are simply flakes who have done no soul-searching or have not suffered in reaching such a heart-wrenching decision.

It makes me see red.

Do so-called pro-lifers ever address the *fathers* who helped create this new life? Do they address the fathers who violated their daughters, or the uncles, or boyfriends, next-door neighbors, coaches, therapists, or priests?

Do any pro-lifers adopt children unwanted by some twelve or

thirteen-year-old girl who hasn't even learned to care for herself, let alone a baby, but is rejected by her family that shames her and disowns her?

How about adopting a child born with fetal alcohol syndrome or drugs transmitted from their mothers' bodies?

No; they merely pray outside the clinic, where everyone can see what righteous, pious people they are.

I've been around the block. Woman gets pregnant; man splits. Woman uses diaphragm but forgot jelly; man blames her. Man says, "I'll pull out in time." But doesn't. Man says he had malaria and is sterile, but isn't. Man doesn't want to use condom as it doesn't feel as good. Man doesn't get vasectomy, because he wants to *know* he *can* get someone pregnant even if he doesn't want or plan to. Man refuses to acknowledge his child.

Man innocently asks, "Don't you trust me?"

Are you kidding?

Life is sacred, unless you're fighting in a war. Life is sacred, unless you have cancer and no insurance to be treated.

And on and on *ad infinitum.*

THE PROFESSOR

AROUND 1970, MY MORNINGS consisted of rising, putting on the coffee, and studying until Anthony woke up. Then he had to get dressed and have breakfast. At three, he took more time putting on his belt and his shirt (all by himself!) than I did dressing, making the beds, and putting breakfast on the table. Then we had to have our time to read together, which involved my reciting the stories while he ate breakfast and I did dishes. If I got distracted, as I sometimes did, I would hear, "Read!" and I'd continue with the story. Then I had to get Anthony to preschool and get to class on time.

Then a French professor came into my life.

Before I met him, I had been minding my own business, quietly operating in my little puddle, and phasing out of an uncommunicative relationship with my good-looking Mexican gardener named José. This French professor was a bit more verbal.

At fifty-three, he was aging gracefully in spite of thin, wavy, graying hair and having to wear a back brace, and he was proud of his legs, which seemed to have dazzled many women when he was on the tennis courts. His first marriage, to an aristocratic Polish intellectual, had produced a son, now a director of plays and films in New York. His second wife, a beautiful woman, had left him in New Mexico; she'd run off with a man on a motorcycle. He had told her, as he had told others, me included, "I picked you up out of the gutter."

From his third wife he had a daughter whom he rarely saw.

The wife would not allow her to write him. Then there was Edda, his German lover, who had left him during his recovery from back surgery. Following Edda there had been a wealthy woman, Enid Bliss, who tried to buy him along with her supply of alcohol, something he remembered with trepidation when passing a certain area on Highway 101, south of Santa Barbara.

MARC J. TEMMER

I met the University of California French professor on a sunny Sunday afternoon on the beach and park area along Cabrillo Boulevard, when I was with my son Anthony and participating in Luis Goena's folk dancing group. When people attended with small children, Luis often put them on his shoulders and kept dancing, which thrilled the children and freed the mothers to dance. For me, it was therapeutic in my declining relationship with José, who had then worked briefly for the Department of Public Works: "I am a garbage man," he would say, "but my body is clean."

The landlady of the small complex where I lived had needed a gardener, so I'd recommended José. With only a fourth-grade education in Mexico, he could remember the days and hours he worked for people without needing to write anything down. I don't have a clue how he filed his income tax—if he ever did, since he was paid mostly in cash, no doubt under the table, but I did admire his memory. I later referred to him as a good-looking S.O.B., but at the time I met the professor, I was still spending some time with him. So that sunny September Sunday on the beach on palm tree-lined Cabrillo Boulevard, across the street from the Santa Barbara Inn and the Child's Estate Zoo, Marc J. Temmer struck up a conversation with me.

"I'm a professor of French literature at UCSB," he told me.

"Oh, I was a French major in college," I said, "but I haven't been speaking and don't remember much now."

"I never do, either," he replied in an offhand way-which made me think he wasn't going to be judgmental.

"I am mostly a poet. I pussyfoot around Europe in the summers and visit my mother in Switzerland. I was born in New York, but my parents were Hungarian Jews. My father died when I was quite young, so I didn't get to know him. We went to Switzerland shortly after I was born. When World War II broke out, since I was Jewish, my mother sent me back to the States, which was a safer option for me; I was seventeen and alone. It wasn't easy. I was lonely: I rented a room in a boarding house near a railroad track and felt even more lonely when I heard the train whistle at night. Then I joined the army, where I got a salary and a meal. After I did my time, I went to Yale, got my doctorate in French literature, and landed the professorship. I was instrumental in bringing a couple to the French Department, M. and Mme. de Lattre, but they turned around and stabbed me in the back. I am planning to sue the University. I have already written and spoken to the Regents of the

University of California."

I had thus received a lot of information about this man in a short time, and was glad to be talking to somebody who was verbal. He seemed quite taken with Anthony, which I also liked. That same day at the beach, he met another single woman with two children, took both our phone numbers, and called us both.

She wasn't interested in him, she told me later. I went on a date with him to the movies. It was nice to be taken on a real, conventional date and talk about a variety of things. I can still picture him waiting for me to return from the ladies room, standing under the street light outside the Granada Theater on State Street, tall, graceful, in his knee-length black trench coat.

He invited me to dinner at his apartment and cooked the whole thing for me, it seemed with some urgency, bringing me a plate of steak, *al dente* asparagus, croissants, and for dessert, strawberry crepes, while I sat on a chaise longue, all to classical music; he liked to compare the viola to a shapely contralto, immersing himself in the rhythm and pitch of the rich chords, moving his hands as if he were the conductor, wanting me to watch him. He talked about his recovery from the back surgery, when his wife and lover had abandoned him, his wife taking their daughter. And how his lover, Edda, had left too, and about how only the music gave him comfort and respite from his pain. He hadn't played tennis after the surgery and complained about having to wear a lumbo-sacral corset, keeping his back straight as if standing at attention all day every day, and about the girls who would come into his office for a conference, some to lie down on the cot there, hoping to get an "A".

In the meantime, José came to my door one last time after finishing his yard work. We both also knew something would change, that our relationship would end. We made love, and though it was unspoken, we both knew it was good-bye. I said I didn't have protection. He said he "wouldn't finish." I sensed that he, too, was seeing someone else.

Several weeks went by. I spoke with Marc on the phone, had dinner with him, and we walked on the beach. He took Anthony to the Vedanta Temple in the foothills of Santa Barbara and loved introducing him, in his cowboy boots and hat, to the monks. And, unsurprisingly, he stayed over one Sunday night. It was a very pleasant night and first morning breakfast after making love for the first time—until I heard the motor of a lawn mower revving up.

"Oh, my God," I exclaimed. "It's Monday morning, and José is here!" Marc knew I had been seeing him and had an ex-husband who lived around the corner, but this turn was a bit of a surprise. Marc's car was parked on the curb in front near the house, and there was no back door to my little home, only a window in my downstairs bathroom and another in the kitchen. What to do? Marc, with back and brace, and wearing good shoes and neat pants, shirt, and jacket, climbed out the kitchen window and, with back and brace, jumped to the ground, which was perpendicular to the back of the next door neighbor's back door. I looked out the front window and saw his station wagon driving away.

Around five o'clock, he returned, highly amused (at first). "I told a colleague of mine that I had to escape out the back window of a woman's house to avoid the gardener! Ha ha ha!" and then: "I'm a full professor! I have to hide from a *gardener?* How would you like it if you spent the night with me and then had to hide in the closet to avoid the *maid?* That's preposterous! A full professor sneaking out a window to avoid the gardener! That could have ruined my back, Mrs. Pussyfoot." I couldn't say anything, so I didn't.

The following Sunday night, Marc spent the night again, without remembering José would be there Monday morning. And once again, we heard the lawn mower revving up.

"I'm not jumping out the window with my bad back again!" Marc said. What to do? This time, he hurried out the front door to the street through the alley on the left side of the front house by a neighbor's fence, avoiding the driveway and the man with the mower.

After I got dressed, I went out and said good morning to José. He was hoping for some sex. However, I could tell from his demeanor, and from what I had learned from his ex-wife, that having sex with more than one woman was something that fed his *macho* ego, so I refrained. We had, anyway, already said our nonverbal good-byes.

When Marc came by again, he was more indignant and less amused.

Another week went by, and another Sunday night with Marc staying over. This time he walked out the front door and down the driveway in full view of José, who, Marc said later, looked startled. When I later came outside, José's first words were: "How could you do this to me?"

Then Marc insisted that I go to José's place and tell him to come later in the day. I thought that was unnecessarily humiliating, but Marc was never anyone to avoid asking for what he wanted.

There were times when Larry came in and went immediately to the bathroom, not to relieve himself but to look in the mirror. Marc compared this behavior to dogs leaving their calling cards on trees or fire hydrants: "Hey, guys, I'm here. This used to be my territory."

One Saturday afternoon, Marc asked me to go with him to the Vedanta Temple. He wanted to take my picture with a nice background. I had kept a blue bridesmaid's dress from a friend's wedding and wore that. However, I was beginning to feel tired, and started getting circles under my eyes. Marc noticed it. "You're pregnant."

"Yes, I am. I am going to have an abortion." It wasn't Marc, who had had a vasectomy. Then I had to tell José I was pregnant. He told me it was my fault and made no attempt to pay for half or take me to or from the hospital. I didn't ask. Marc picked me up after it was over and took me home. Needless to say, he was not fond of José.

After a while, either José quit or the landlady let him go.

The following summer, Marc went to Europe, as usual, and came back with interesting stories, a favorite being that he had met a woman who was a lion tamer, and that the Italians were so charming, even though they were all crooks, and how much better things were done in Europe. "Here, the young people I see come from wealthy families, but they ape poverty." (I don't know how aware he was of the cultural and communal life espoused by the hippies in the '60s, though he was fully aware of the burning of the Bank of America in Isla Vista. Later he changed his clean-cut appearance for sandals, a beard, and a back pack when he married wife number five, a student.

Usually, when Marc returned from Europe, he found a room to rent; he didn't need much, since he was at the University or out "pussyfooting" more than he was in. On his return this time, he seemed to have trouble finding a place, and then asked if he could bring his music player to my place. He said, "I have never been happier than when I am in your run-down dump."

I was getting a bit uncomfortable with such talk, as much as I appreciated his fondness for Anthony and his enjoying grocery shopping for me, throwing in an occasional can of octopus tentacles and asking me if he had "chosen well." He loved sitting at my kitchen table opposite the old-fashioned ice box and writing poetry, mostly in French, throwing in some German words and English as well. I didn't like the way he moved in with me, though. I didn't doubt he cared for me but worried that being in a committed relationship with him would take my youth away. I was thirty-three, and he was fifty-one. He had set ways and feared getting old. Telling Anthony not to get his dirty shoes (on three-year-old feet) on the car upholstery was just one example.

Marc did enjoy entertaining, and we had people to dinner (in my dump), and sometimes he'd call me and triumphantly announce, "We're invited!" I enjoyed his friends, who were well-read and cultured people. One couple was in the Linguistics Department at UCSB, and I later took a class with Edith Traeger Johnson, the wife. I met others from the Classics and Spanish Departments and the French Department, as well as Icarus, a Greek, who described Marc as someone who could verbally appeal to women's sexual fantasies but couldn't follow through physically because of his bad back. Not completely true, but he did give that impression. Consider one of Marc's poems for Sheldon Kaganoff, a pottery teacher from New Jersey:

> *Did you ever, Kaganoff, dream a dream*
> *to love a woman never seen?*

comparing Kaganoff, the potter, to Pygmalian, the sculptor.

Marc helped me go through the process of applying to UCSB for my teacher's credential, but when I was actually in school and studying, he would expect me to give him my full attention whenever he came in. And he would ask me to draw him a bath: "In Europe it's a sign of love," he would tell me.

"Well, here it's a sign of subservience," I would answer.

And he also suggested that he teach me elocution. I read from Milton, but he would have me do it in the older, more stilted style of ministers' sermons. After three sessions of that, I called it quits. He enjoyed, and was good at, starting a discussion and manipulating the conversation to get you to say something you didn't agree with. And he loved snapping his fingers, hoping that you would, like a dog, put your hands in front of you as if begging for a biscuit. He told his friends about the time he said, "Coo to me, baby." To which I answered, "Get yourself a turtle dove." He knew how to get you so angry you wanted to commit murder, as when he corrected my grammar in the middle of an argument. In these cases, my way of dealing with him was to shout and swear. For some reason, that intimidated him and he would back off. Once he wanted to take Anthony and me to Disneyland, hoping that we would see him as the "Papa Bear" and play up to that game. I had an uncomfortable feeling when we started out in his impeccably clean station wagon.

As we were approaching the area where he had lived with Enid Bliss, he said, "Talk to me." I drew a blank. He complained that I didn't divert his attention from those memories.

We got to Disneyland and walked around. He started complaining that I, in particular, wasn't kissing up to him as the papa bear. He got angry. I got angry and started yelling and swearing, until he said, "Look at poor Anthony. He doesn't know what to make of this." And of course a few heads turned to see what the noise was about.

He sometimes suggested that I "park" Anthony at my sister's in Hawaii, or with my parents or brother, so he could take me to Europe. I found that presumptuous. He also talked of getting married. I refused on both counts. By the end of that school year, I asked him to leave, knowing he had a place to sleep in his office and knew the drill for finding a room if he needed one. I remember the night he left, sadly walking down the driveway with his briefcase, going to his office. He later told me, and others, I'd kicked him out without any food. When at first I told my mother about his liking to shop, she said drily, "That's the least he can do." The point was well taken.

Marc later stayed with a couple with whom we had shared meals, a Swedish woman named Birghitta and her second husband. He was depressed; I went to dinner there on Birghitta's invitation but was uncomfortable, as he was quite silent and at one point turned to me abruptly and stared. But he got over it and went on to have a Mrs. Temmer, number four, whom I became close friends with, a Swiss woman who spoke English, French, and German, taught piano, and helped him with his French and German poetry while also not appreciating his snap fingers/beg for biscuit game or being told she had been picked up out of the gutter. Then there were student/wife number five and wife number six, a Swiss woman who married him and got her green card.

To my knowledge, he never succeeded in suing the University of California. I would occasionally run into him. One New Year's Eve, when I was dating Raoul, we went to Greti's (my friend and wife number four, but it was not a good mix with the men: one, the educated intellectual opening up a discussion of politics; the other, a short, gritty Mexican who had to hustle for survival). Even though Marc sometimes (purposefully) irritated me to the point of my wanting to commit murder, I can say that I appreciate his showing me the process of writing, something I didn't get across to Raoul when he wanted to write about his time in Chino. I wonder if he ever got his book finished, or published.

MY MUSIC MUSES

O N THE MEMORABLE DAY when I realized everything in my life was wrong, I sat in my bathtub and cried hysterically, then lay in the sun on the roof of my little house in back, realizing that I wanted to have a child. I also realized that I could not go back to New Jersey, except for vacations, unless I had a profession that I was good at and an avocation that I was good at and committed to. Regarding the latter, I wanted to sing and to be able to deliver a song that grabbed people's attention by the truth of the message. No matter what it was. So began the journey of what I did for love—not fame or money—but for love, joy, and to be the best that I could be; teaching was an offshoot of that.

I started in a choral class with the excellent adult education program in Santa Barbara, this one taught by Charles Gallagher, who had been in the music/jazz field for decades and knew his trade. Charlie, as we called him, was in his late sixties, I'd guess—lean, white-haired, low-keyed, with a gentle sense of humor. He was the most healthy diabetic I have ever seen. He walked every day, had steak for breakfast, and was religious about his diet. Once when I had invited him and his wife Norma to dinner, and I asked him if there was anything he couldn't have or needed to have, he simply said, "Oh, plan to have whatever you like. I'll eat what I am able to eat of the meal." He was a role model for diabetics!

Another member of Charlie's class was Alberta Brown, twenty or so years my senior, who had worked in Admissions at Pembroke and whose sister now lived at Valle Verde, a lovely retirement community in Santa Barbara. Alberta had bought a house near Santa Barbara High School but would, in time, move in with the sister. She had a rich contralto voice, whereas I was a mezzo soprano. We sang some duets, two of which were "I Waited for the Lord" and "O Tannenbaum." That was almost fifty years ago, but I have a recording of the former song and can say now that we weren't too shabby!

Mrs. Lura Dolas was my first and major vocal teacher, in that she taught me how to project without a microphone, how to breathe (essential when singing Handel, which I cut my teeth on). She was like a mentor; she took me to some musical programs that she got complimentary tickets for—some concerts at which, if she heard or saw something a bit off, she'd give me a little nudge and point it out to me. She was an admired and respected institution in Santa Barbara because she loved her work and her students, and she spent many hours helping the youth theatre program and other musical organizations in town. She was professional and savvy. She believed that, when she had a student, he or she was *hers*. Occasionally, that mind-set caused me some stress, as when she got angry because I took an adult ed class with a male teacher new to the scene, Richard Weiss. Weiss had a technique she found invalid:

Put a cork between your teeth and make a screech-like noise (like a baby crying), and he fancied himself a debonair bachelor around town, thereby attracting many women on the rebound who wanted to emote but had little vocal training; occasionally that got him in trouble, as he was in a relationship with my friend Rosalie, who was his right-hand person, as I had been with Richard Nelson, the producer of the Santa Barbara Playhouse. Sometimes chuckling about the drama of *her* situation relieved the tension I was feeling in the dysfunctional relationship *I* was in!

Once, Mrs. Dolas ran into Richard Weiss at a supermarket, and they stopped to speak to each other. Richard said something about my needing to bring my voice more forward (believing his cork method could no doubt do that); Mrs. Dolas was thoroughly disgusted with his arrogance, his crude vocabulary, and his pretension. He often used big words incorrectly to impress, to the entertainment of some of us.

Yet, though Mrs. Dolas did think poorly of him, she later acknowledged that the exposure had been good for me. And she taught me a method for phrasing that I could adapt to teaching English as a Second Language. So when singing in German, which I didn't know, she would put a pencil to the page of music and draw curves indicating what word led to the next important word to stress. That process gave clarity to the phrase and the whole sentence. I was proud to be able to do the same thing when helping students read their compositions out loud.

As time went on, however, my limited time (I had enrolled at UCSB to get my teacher's credential) and income caused me to cut back on my lessons. Mrs. Dolas offered to teach me for free, but I didn't feel comfortable with that, so I tapered off.

IT WAS SEVERAL YEARS before I took lessons again, and that was after I started dating Dick Galway. He and his son had both studied with Mrs. Dolas for a while, but Dick and Mrs. Dolas weren't in tune with each other. Dick, then divorced, liked being a gallant man about town, which she felt a bit put off by, and he wanted to swing a bit more, so he started taking lessons from another seasoned teacher and wonderful human being, Sharon Courrier. She worked with many students who were in shows, sometimes opera, but more often musicals and more current forms of musical entertainment. While Mrs. Dolas stopped doing recitals at the Woman's Club, Sharon had soirees at her home.

I started in time to notice that the wide range I sang as a mezzo was diminishing from lack of practice. And so, one Valentine's Day, Dick gave me a card offering four lessons with Sharon. She was a bit younger than Mrs. Dolas and had been married to a Mr. Robert McDavid, a local play director. She also had a son named Jimmy, who was a talented dancer without ever having had a dance lesson. She was short and blonde and had been involved in theater productions and a children's opera when married to McDavid. Her method of teaching vocal exercises was different from that of Mrs. Dolas, partly because, in using a microphone, one didn't need to project the voice in the same way.

Meanwhile, one of Mrs. Dolas's students, Ed Cooke, a nephew of Dick Galway, worked in the local junk yard in high school and would come for his lessons wearing his junkyard jumpsuit; he was tall and lanky and also played a hilarious Snoopy scrunched up on top of (Snoopy's) doghouse. He married a singer, and they went on to New York and probably Europe.

Sharon also had a student named Ed, or Eduardo Villa, who also went on to New York and Europe to perform.

Then there was Mirth Hammerberg. Mirth played the piano for Richard Weiss and for some adult education classes, and later for *Singer's Showcase,* a group of singers who prepared songs to sing at retirement and nursing homes. Mirth was a short, heavy woman with white hair in a pony tail, and, because of arthritis, her head seemed tilted to one side when she didn't wear a neck brace. She could play in any key, though when older she sometimes absent-mindedly switched keys, causing the singer to scramble to find the new notes! I joined the group. We would go to her house and work on four songs for ten dollars an hour. The grand piano was in her living room, near sliding doors opening up onto a patio and a small shed where her husband, Ed, painted many desert scenes and some Alaskan ones. Mirth was exposed to music early in life at school, where her talents were recognized, and later, she played for school programs and musicals when her adopted daughter, Carol, was in school in Santa Barbara.

She bemoaned the fact that so much music was cut out of school programs in later years. I do as well. The first time I met Mirth, at one of Weiss's musical events, she invited me to come to her house and bring music. I was excited about doing that. It was after we spent an hour together that she asked for the ten dollars she hadn't mentioned before the session. Singers paid to work with an accompanist, and then sang for free at retirement and nursing homes.

Many years later, after Ed and Carol had died, I went to visit

Mirth, and we did sing for fun—no charge! But when I admired
one of Ed's paintings on the wall, and she asked me if I'd like it, I
thought, Why not? I offered to give her some cash for it and asked
how much it might be worth (some people never learn). She told
me six hundred dollars. At the time I was not strapped for money,
since my financial situation had changed after moving back to New
Jersey. So I gave her the money and gave my son the picture, and
I don't know what happened to it; he didn't hold onto unnecessary
things.

Then there was Elizabeth Layton, who, with her then husband
Ken, produced a dinner show, *A Dickens of a Christmas*, on a yearly
basis. As long as it lasted it was an institution. Though I didn't
participate in it, many of my singing friends did. She was a wonderful comedic singer; she also took over the opera workshop with
Adult Education after the previous director, Timothy Fetler, retired.
She taught a class on preparing for auditions and mentioned that,
when younger and going to Los Angeles to audition, she would always pass a spot on Highway 101 and have to get out to throw up
due to the degree of anxiety she was experiencing. Basically, she
taught us to go through the routine of walking on stage, giving our
music to the accompanist, standing stage center, putting our hands
together, and saying, "I am _____(name) and I am going to
sing _____(name of song).

Elizabeth's husband, Ken, wasn't very nice to her and fooled
around; eventually they got divorced. When she directed the final
performance of *A Dickens of a Christmas*, he came in to disrupt one
of the rehearsals and she had to get a restraining order on him. Ken
was something of an arrogant prima donna, and Elizabeth was a

compassionate person; she once noticed in a restaurant that the man in the next booth was bullying his female partner, and when she went to the rest room, Elizabeth also went in and asked her if she was all right and whether she needed any help.

Mme. Elizabeth, as she was sometimes called, did have a comic streak. She did the duet "Libiamo" from *La Traviata*, for example, and she and her partner wound up being sloshed by the end of the song, she drinking, not from the glass, but from the bowl. Or, when telling us about one of the reviewers from the *Santa Barbara News-Press* who liked the ladies. He always tried to kiss whomever he had invited to accompany him to review a show; she, in telling us she was going, imitated a young teen-age girl nervously twitching her lips, afraid and shy in anticipating her first sensual experience!

Elizabeth was unable to make enough in the music industry, so she took on a daytime job with handicapped children at an institution. This gave her retirement and health benefits. She was loved and respected there in a way that she was not always resd-pected in the music/theater world.

I met Alice McCarter at one of the singing events organized by Richard Weiss. Alice came from "Missoura," and her husband, Fred, worked at the Department of Welfare, as did Larry, my ex. Alice could sight-read almost anything. The reason? When she practiced the piano when young, she got out of doing the dishes! She had big brown eyes, a warm smile, and from her emanated a feeling of well-being. This was because, even when going through some of the ups and downs in her life—and I met her just before she separated from Fred—she seemed grounded and took the time to regroup after any kind of upset. When she was first separated, she and I went out to a cocktail lounge in Montecito, where a friend of hers was playing. As we entered the room, several male heads turned. Before looking for a place to sit, we went to the ladies' room. As soon as we came out, one man ushered us to seats he had found and joined us. I, then divorced for a few years, had already gotten defensive about guys trying to hit on me, but Alice simply laughed her way through the evening, which certainly helped me to loosen up. When one of the men said something she felt inappropriate, she paused in time to choose the words that would tell him in no uncertain terms that his behavior was unacceptable. In short, she was a good role model for me in that respect.

Alice had two children: Kaitlin, the older of the two and a year or so older than Anthony; and Brad, a year or two younger than Anthony. We spent time together with and without our children. Alice had been in therapy, so that when she and Fred separated, she had thought through her decision and was sure of it. I realized that I was in need of therapy, because the triangle I was in was becoming destructive. I asked her about her therapist. Her description went something like this:

"With Irwin, you pay—it's not cheap. But he expects you to work, and he expects to get results. He doesn't mince words, but he has a great sense of humor, which really worked for me. He's from New York, and he's tough-minded. When he plays racquet ball, he plays for blood. I know that because a friend of mine plays the game and knows him."

I figured that description would work for me, so I called and made an appointment. His office was in a comfortable room attached to his home, on a large piece of property in Montecito. I entered the room and saw a wiry man of average height with salt-and-pepper hair, a mustache, and a slight New York accent, and was invited to sit on a black leather couch while he sat opposite me in a matching leather chair. A bookcase ran across one wall; one book, about dream therapy, caught my attention, and I later borrowed it.

He asked me about myself and why I was there, and I mentioned my being a single parent and the Dick/Elliott triangle I was in that was causing me despair. Physically, I was having digestive issues; emotionally, I was stressed, impatient with my son, and depressed. On beginning to answer one question, I started to cry. One of his first gems of wisdom was, "Your job is to feel good about yourself." Next: "We're here to attack problems." (Mental racquet ball! I liked it, though it was sometimes tough.) On another occasion, I asked him, "If you have thoughts about jumping off an overpass onto the freeway, is that suicidal?" He looked at me significantly and nodded. Thanks to the three years with Irwin and his terse advice, I was able to move on.

WITH ALICE AND ANOTHER FRIEND who was part of Weiss's Singers' Showcase, we enjoyed many years of camaraderie in various musical productions. Afterwards, we sometimes went to listen to our friend, Al Reese, who played in many of the lounges in Santa Barbara: the Santa Barbara Inn, the Biltmore, Tommy's Golden Cock, the Tee-Off, and the Miramar, to name a few.

And Alice, once when we were at Tommy's Golden Cock, saw someone she had previously worked for, Vivien Irene, who was with her brother, John, and as the three were chatting, Irene suggested that Alice spend the weekend with them on an occasion. Whereupon, Alice said to John, "If we're going to be sleeping together, we might as well have a dance tonight." That comment was the beginning of their relationship, which ended in marriage after both sold their respective homes and bought a house together. They have been there ever since. Alice McCarter became Alice Bourland.

When I began to date Dick Galway, I met another pianist through the singles group at the Unitarian Church, Jean Olson, and we worked on numerous show tunes for events at the church. On a Sunday where church members were supposed to pledge how they would contribute to the church, I sang "Pennies from Heaven" and "Money Makes the World Go Round" from *Cabaret*, not the typical church anthem, to be sure!

Both Alice and Jean were friends with whom I could share my frustrations in some of my relationships. One evening, when I was particularly wound up on the way to listen to Al, Alice said, "Don't fight it." That was all I needed to return to calm! Jean just spent time with me going to local festivals, which was enough of a distraction to help me to regroup.

Another friend I met through *Singer's Showcase* was Joan Brienzo, a mezzo with a natural voice, divorced with two children. Joan, Alice, and I often went out to sing and listen to Al. Sometimes Alice played when Al took a break, though her music was more classical. Often a listener would buy us a drink. I learned that more than one drink caused me to be sloppy when singing, so I told the waitress to change the drink to club soda. On one occasion, when I played one of the nuns in *Soeur Angelica*, I had a sore throat and had a little tequila before performing, and then was so worried I'd miss my one liner, "See that your hearing and words are fraught with quiet and humble submission," that I was flat, and Mme. Elizabeth Layton was not happy.

During those years, I didn't have much money, and we were all struggling and finding our own ways, but they were rich years that we look back on, sometimes giving thanks that our children survived those times, and remembering the good fellowship and the focus on our mutual love of music.

AND THEN THERE WAS RICK

I T MUST HAVE BEEN AROUND 1976, when my son Anthony was about nine and I had been divorced for about seven years, that we moved from a charming, run-down place behind a quaint house with four rented apartments: from 410 ½ West Sola, to 1109 San Pascual, Apartment 3, in Santa Barbara, California.

Anthony's father, Larry, lived around the corner with his brother, Frank, on Euclid Avenue, a short road parallel to Highway 101.

I was dating the Hungarian French professor eighteen years my senior at that time, though our relationship didn't continue. But he helped me move, not by any means of lifting heavy boxes and furniture into the apartment—but by asking other people to. He had a bad back and wasn't shy, as I was, about asking people for help.

Anthony and I moved over the freeway to 1109 San Pascual, Apartment 3, on a road, also parallel to 101, that intersected at Mission Street, then Micheltorena, then Carrillo, and down to Ortega. A sociologist might have called that area in Santa Barbara a lower middle class or an upper lower class area. The first neighbor I met was Rick, who was the same age as Anthony, though he attended a different school. I saw this skinny kid with fine blond hair, parted in the middle and grown down to his jaw, just as he finished poking a hole in the screen of my living room window. I knocked on the door of Apartment 2, introduced myself to his mother, Susan, and told her what he'd done. She reprimanded him.

The apartment manager was Wayne, a heavy-set man with a big authoritative voice who told his three kids to "set to" if they dragged their feet when doing their chores or other things he ordered. He had a gun in his apartment but didn't find occasion to use it while we lived there, although he occasionally threatened to. He lived in Apartment 4, on the other side of mine.

Susan and Tony Briggs, her significant other, were first cousins. Susan's two children, Robin and Rick, came from somewhere in the mid-West, as did Tony; the kids' father wound up in Florida, I learned later.

One might have guessed that Susan and Tony were related: They were both short and had short haircuts, hers blond, his brown, both wavy and parted on one side; their faces were square, their eyebrows elegantly arched. They both wore slacks, mostly corduroy, and turtleneck sweaters, though sometimes Tony wore a short-sleeved cotton shirt with a pocket over the left breast. He was an artist, a painter of outdoor scenes, and his specialty was redwoods. Susan was an excellent photographer but did not work at it professionally. She chose instead to keep the home fires burning.

Her daughter, Robin, was also blond, spunky, and athletic. When she started junior high and got interested in school plays, she wanted to be an actress; she would call me and offer to mop my floor in exchange for singing lessons, though getting her to find the correct note was a challenge.

Anthony and Rick became friends, even if I took a dim view of some of their activities, such as trying to light the threads in our shag rug, or hiding a *Playboy* magazine in Anthony's mattress, or hiding cigarettes in his closet. No doubt he thought that he would get into less trouble in Apartment 3 than he would in Apartment 2 and attract *Tony's* attention.

What I enjoyed doing with both of them was practicing drum rhythms on our makeshift kitchen table. Anthony took drum classes at school for a while, and we got a deal on a set.

Rick had some kind of learning disability, and since it was not addressed in any positive way, he ultimately fell through the cracks. He liked animals and spent part of one summer feeding the ones at Santa Barbara's Child's Estate. Life for this family had its hardships.

ONE NIGHT, WHEN TONY WAS AWAY, there was a fierce hurricane. When I got home from teaching my ESL class, the three remaining Briggses were in my living room, sitting on sheets, having gotten the creeps during the storm. After I chatted with them for a while, they dared to return to their apartment.

Tony, an artist and the family breadwinner, didn't make much money, and Susan, a talented photographer, preferred to be a stay-at-home mom. Tony would take his paintings to sell at the beach—many of them depicting redwoods in northern California, to earn his living. His paintings were beautiful—grand, shimmering red-brown tree trunks rising to the top of the canvas, occasional sun rays shining through them, ground foliage enough to bring you into the scene but not enough to distract from the red-brown majesty. Women would steal to get that color in their hair!

One Sunday afternoon after Tony had been at the beach, peddling his wares, he showed me one in particular and said, "Natalie, I think I have outdone myself on this!" He was proud and rightly so. It was beautiful. He was wearing his plaid slacks and short-sleeved shirt. I can still see him and hear the humorous tone in his raspy voice.

IT WAS MY BIRTHDAY—not that I gave a shit. My son was about eleven; I was teaching part-time at Santa Barbara City College (SBCC) and studying in graduate school at UCSB. I didn't make enough money to pay the rent. I didn't have time for my kid, and I had a bunch of homework to do on that nice, warm, sunny afternoon.

Anthony went down the street to play with Rick. His mom and surrogate father, Tony, had found a small house to rent at a reasonable price—not easy in Santa Barbara. It had a small porch and even a back door! And, so typically in Santa Barbara, it was all on one floor, a modest but practical two-bedroom. Take a rectangle twice as long as it is wide; in one half you have two bedrooms separated by a bathroom, and in the other half you have the living room and kitchen with a small coat closet in between, but unlike their house, my apartment had no back door. The saving feature was that the windows in each room were long and horizontal, slid open, and brought in a lot of light. I am partial to wide windows, even when the only view is of another building and a driveway.

I was at my all-purpose, bridge-sized kitchen table, trying to make a bell-curve for stats, when the phone rang.

"Hullo," I said aloofly.

A voice, raspy from smoking, cavernous from a cleft palate, greeted me. "Hello, Natalie, this is Tony."

"I know your voice, Tony."

"What are you doing?" he asked.

"I have an assignment due next Friday, and it's taking forever."

"How about taking a little break and coming down here for a half hour?"

"Thanks, but I haven't come to a stopping point yet, and I'm not sure when I will."

"Okay, I'll check back with you."

That continued. Pretty soon, Susan called and asked if I would like to come and have a coffee break. Then Tony again.

"*Ooooookay*, I'll be down in a half hour."

"Guess I did need a break," I told myself as I walked the couple of blocks down San Pascual, the same street as mine but below Carrillo, an exit street from the busy freeway. It was warm as I strolled past Carrillo, which on its right curved up a hill to the Mesa, which took you to the ocean, and the view of sea and sky was always spectacular—and so close to my apartment! A few blocks to the left, and you were in busy downtown Santa Barbara. I passed numerous apartments and small houses, quite plain, but with a smattering of palm trees, some rose bushes, one or two avocado trees, and dust. Larry, my ex, used to say, "If you're gonna be poor, be poor in California, not in New York." We did not argue on that point.

I knocked on their door, and Susan invited me into their small, square kitchen; on the red-checked linoleum tablecloth sat a carrot loaf-cake with butter cream icing. I was relieved it was small cake. I can get hooked on them. Plates and napkins, forks and spoons, were all ready, and coffee cups and glasses for soda. With happy smiles, they sang "Happy Birthday" to me.

YEARS LATER, TONY REMINDED ME of this time and of how I had politely listened to the song in my honor and shared the food and fellowship with them, "politely tolerating it," I think he said. They'd planned it when Anthony told them it was my birthday. Another friend remarked to me several times that Anthony had a sweetness about him. So true, even when, at age forty-two, he could visit and still polish off a container of frozen yogurt and leave it under his bed!

The Briggses must have had some other kind of income just to pay the rent; I never knew where it came from, other than what Tony made selling his paintings; in any case, they remained there for about a year before leaving for Grass Valley, where they'd previously lived and could do so more cheaply.

ABOUT THREE YEARS LATER, Susan, Tony, and Rick returned to Santa Barbara to look for Robin, who had run away. Susan told me that both Rick and Robin had moved out of their home in Grass Valley but had no money, and, when found, were living on potato soup.

They did find Robin, and I offered to have her stay with me if she wanted to remain in Santa Barbara. "Thank you," Susan told me, "but I'm afraid that she would just live on the streets." So back they all went to Grass Valley for a while. As it turned out, my taking her in would not have been a good idea for me; the belief that she would live in the street became a reality.

Another year or so had passed when I received a call from Susan. "Rick and I are coming back to Santa Barbara, and could we stay with you for about two weeks?"

Anthony had just started ninth grade at San Marcos High School. I had some reservations, which were unfounded. I would be busy and so wouldn't be a good hostess, but Susan was a good housekeeper and an easy guest. I enjoyed her company and missed our conversations when they later found a place. Single parents need like minds, and though not ambitious, Susan was intelligent, and that intelligence came out later.

While with me, she slept on the couch, and Rick slept in Anthony's room. Sue registered Rick at San Marcos; after a few days, though, he refused to go. He then tried Santa Barbara High School—also a no-go. It was not a place he wanted to be; even without the learning disability he could not relate to the usual school culture. In the meantime, Susan had found a small train car in a mobile home park in Carpentaria, south of Santa Barbara, where some of her artist friends lived.

One day, when Rick was still trying out school, I drove him and Anthony to the mobile park. When we got to their trailer, Anthony uttered a chuckle. I glared at him; fortunately, he didn't continue.

One evening, Sue and I went to a Holly Near concert at the Arlington Theater, a large, Spanish style space with its ceiling painted like the sky. We got there early, sat down, and chatted; looking around, she said, "Well, this is overwhelming!"

"What's overwhelming?" I asked.

"Everyone here is lesbian," she said.

"They are?" I looked around. The large theater wasn't half full, but there were mostly women sitting in twos, threes, or clusters.

"Of course."

". . .How do you know?"

"Well, I'm a lesbian," she said.

I was completely taken aback. I had several good friends who were lesbians, and it didn't bother me in any way, but Sue had had the father of her children and then lived with Tony! And upon her return to this area, her closest friend was a man who lived in the same trailer park. I was at a loss for words. That was the end of that conversation.

Once they got settled, we didn't see as much of them. Rick went to an alternative school for a spell, but I don't know for how long. As time went on, he got into drinking and drugs. One day about a year or two later, I saw in the distance—when I was at the beach of the Biltmore Hotel in Montecito—a skinny blond kid walking along the railroad track, and knew it was Rick, a little taller, his fine hair longer as well, and unkempt, holding a brown paper bag. It saddened me.

These people, and their life style, were a far cry from what I, having grown up in the New Jersey suburbs, was accustomed to, but they were real, and they were my friends.

Once in a while, Susan and I got together. She spent a lot of time with Bob, the guitarist friend who lived in the same mobile home park. He knew a lot of songs and could do Spanish songs like a native Mexican with the little sing-song at the end of a musical line. We sang together sometimes. Bob liked to talk, and Susan liked to listen or, more accurately, to be in the background. She was soft-spoken; however, she was not shy about expressing her opinions. She was not naive either. For some years, she suffered from endometriosis, and she had been ignoring it. Finally, she went ahead and had a complete hysterectomy. It was a long and arduous surgery; she was already thin, and she got thinner. A sister came to visit her, and Bob was there along with Barbara, another artist at the trailer park, whom I had met before they all moved north. It was this rowdy group that visited her the night before surgery and later on the day after. Fortunately, we didn't get bounced. In her quiet way, Susan had some kind of endurance. In spite of her thin frame and extensive surgery, she recovered quickly and was soon back in her galley trailer car.

SEVERAL MORE YEARS PASSED. I was still living in my two- bedroom at 1109 San Pascual, and Anthony had by then graduated from San Marcos. While a junior, he had enlisted in the marines, wanting to get a job where he could make a lot of money. He thought becoming a mechanic working on jet planes would be lucrative. His perspective was understandable, since I, a part-time instructor at Santa Barbara City College, could not have afforded to send him to college, and his father's view was, "When you're eighteen, you're on your own, kid." That was how it had been where he grew up on 109th Street between Amsterdam and Columbus, before it became gentrified.

When he became a senior, Anthony changed his mind. Having become successful as a wrestler, he was in demand and had choices. He went to Humboldt State in northern California, and a mentoring coach helped him line up financial aid.

I, in the meantime, continued to take voice lessons and joined several singing classes. I learned that Susan was attending a class with a man who didn't sound like Bob. I think they'd had a falling out. This other man, who was retired or laid off, had been a trouble-shooter for some big company. They stayed in the trailer car, neat and orderly as Sue kept it, and Rick had a job but was staying in the shed on the side of the trailer. Sister Robin was not around. She was known to have gone with a few men who were able to supply her with drugs. During one period she too showed up and stayed in the shed. One day when I was visiting with Sue, she knocked on the shed door and told Robin I was there. She asked if Robin would like to come out and say hello. Robin declined, but when I said hello through the door, she responded in kind. I wasn't surprised, but was glad we could say *something* to each other. It was rumored, though, that at times she got wasted and became violent.

Late one morning, I got a call from Larry, my ex, who worked at the Department of Welfare and asked me if I had heard the news about Rick.

"No. What happened?"

"He was shot in the head by a friend of Susan. Some guy who had been a trouble-shooter for a company and got paranoid about people coming after him. His gun was about a foot away from Rick's head."

"Oh, my God. I have her number. I'll call her."

"It's been in the *Santa Barbara News-Press* and on TV all morning," he added. I found the blurb in the *News-Press* and called Susan.

"It was a bizarre nightmare," she told me. "I had given Rick a restraining order. I felt that he should not be living in that little shack next to the trailer car. I told him it wasn't a healthy situation, and that it'd be better if he rented a place with a friend and had a life on his own, with his peers. Dick, fearful that Robin would show up, had a gun and put it under our pillow. He'd told me that about a week before. The day Rick was going to move out, Rick came to the trailer door to talk me out of it. I called the police, and he stepped on the doorstep and said he wanted to talk to them. Dick got frantic and took out the gun. It was only a foot from Rick's head."

Rick had said to Susan on a few occasions that he had "done good." He had gotten off booze and drugs and gotten a job. He had a job application that required a GED. "The restraining order wasn't a disciplinary measure," she went on, "but because I wanted something better for him."

"Where's his body now?"

"He's at the Haider Mortuary, and there'll be a wake this afternoon and evening and tomorrow morning. We're planning a service at the cemetery just up from the trailer park, tomorrow afternoon."

"I'll be there."

"Thanks, Natalie."

"I'm. . .so sorry this has happened."

"Dick panicked, knowing that Robin was around and could be so violent, and his paranoia that people from his workplace could be looking for retribution just put him over the top. . . ."

I ENTERED ONE OF THE MORTUARY ROOMS, and there was Rick.

He had grown from a skinny, unkempt boy into a beautiful

young man—more filled out, hair trimmed, and was wearing a short blond mustache. I broke down, but for another reason as well: He had a job application that required the GED. I worked with students at Santa Barbara City College in ESL and essential skills, many of whom had come back to school to make up for what they had missed earlier in their lives, many for the same reason Rick had. Some of those students were in recovery or had learning disabilities. I enjoyed working with them, and I would have been most happy to help Rick in that way. If nothing else, I was sure I could have helped him feel better about himself as a student. Having grown up with an intellectual inferiority complex myself, I took great joy in helping people to define what they were good at, and to discover how to build on their strengths to work on their difficulties. Although I was not surprised that he hadn't asked me, I wished he had. Of all people, I would have loved to help him. And it would have been good for me in another way: I was a part-time instructor with no support or validation from the community college bureaucracy, and received minimal wages. My validation came from my colleagues and students. Oddly, just knowing that I could have helped him, even though he was gone, made me feel a bond toward him and sure of my abilities. I stayed there with him and Susan for the evening.

I asked her if she had tried to reach Tony. She said she hadn't felt comfortable enough to do so since their parting. I offered to instead.

When I got home, I found Tony's number in Grass Valley and dialed. He answered.

"Hi, Tony, this is Natalie. How are you?"

"I'm okay," the cavernous rasp answered. "How about you?"

"I'm fine, Tony, but I have some very bad news."

"What happened?"

I explained. "Well, I've had it with Susan. I was the one who raised those kids, like my own, and I can't deal any more with Susan's games." He was *angry*. I didn't ask why but recalled that Anthony had been critical of Sue for having no gumption and not taking any initiative with Robin and Rick, or herself probably. I didn't know about that either, but thought it better not to ask for details.

"Do you want to come down, Tony? Sue is going to have a memorial in the cemetery where he'll be put, and Barbara is having a little reception in her mobile home."

"I'll come down and stay with a friend in Ventura. I'm not going to see Susan, or Robin for that matter. But I'll come down. I got no appreciation at all for raising them, but I'll say goodbye to Rick. Thanks for letting me know, Natalie. I'll see you when I get there."

"Yes, we'll have some catching up to do. I'm sorry for the sad news, and this one is sad. Give me a call when you get here. We can go for lunch or dinner or something. I hope you're still painting."

"Yeah, and it's a lot cheaper to live up here than down there. Too many rich people in Santa Barbara. It's not the life style for me."

"I know what you mean. The service is at 2:00 day after tomorrow. *Ciao*."

We hung up. The phone rang; it was Susan. "Natalie, would

you do me a favor? I was hoping Bob could play his guitar and you could sing 'Just a Closer Walk with Thee.' You'll have time to go over it with him."

"I'd love to. I just hope I don't break down in the middle of it. We'd better go over it tomorrow."

"How about eleven, and then we can go to Carrow's for lunch." I don't think Susan ever had breakfast, but she always had a hamburger and a Coke for lunch. Carrow's was just off the freeway and near the mobile home park.

The next day, Bob and I went over the song; Susan had taken up smoking, which she hadn't done when she was living in Santa Barbara, but Tony smoked, Robin smoked, and probably Rick by then, and Bob smoked. I didn't know about the current boyfriend, who was being held in the Santa Barbara County Jail.

THE CEMETERY WAS ALSO CLOSE to the mobile home park, just a little north on Calle Real and thus easy to find. It was a beautiful day, sunny but not hot. There was a woman preacher Susan knew, and chairs were set up in front of the large open grave. It occurred to me that, if Susan was not what one would describe as a "good" mother, she had done right by him this time. I don't know what the time in the funeral home, the embalming, and the plot had cost, but she'd done it, sadly but well. I don't remember what all the preacher said, but several people spoke, as did I, through tears, saying that of all the people who needed help, Rick would have been the one I would most have liked to help. I didn't see Tony, who stayed way in the background so as not to be seen. There were only a few of Rick's friends; most of the people were friends of Sue at the mobile park.

After the service was over, most everyone went over to Barbara's and we had time to chat over rolls, potato and macaroni salad, cold cuts, Coke and other carbonated beverages, coffee, tea, wine, and cake. Barbara's trailer was quite a lot bigger than Sue's, fortunately, since her husband and son lived there as well. I always got a kick out of Bob, as he was a talker, and amusing even when serious, and most of all was a good musician. After about a half hour, I looked at Susan, who seemed uncomfortable. I raised my eyebrows.

"It seems close in here," she remarked. "Do you want to go back to the cemetery with me?"

"That's a good idea. You'll want to say good-bye more quietly, I think."

Back we went and just sat. Some groundskeepers were mowing a distance away; we were in a quiet, sunny spot with green grass, a blue sky, with the hum of the mowers in the distance.

We just sat for a while. "Well, even though it is in death, you did right by him," I remarked.

"I was afraid Robin might show up, and that worried me. She's hanging out with really bad company, and I was afraid there might be a scene. She's really hooked on drugs."

Robin had been physically active and healthy looking; I couldn't imagine what she might look like now, and I didn't want to find out. I was fond of her, but to see her looking wasted and acting crazily I would just as soon forego. "That's too bad. She had a lot of spunk and promise."

"And now," Susan added, "there will be a hearing for Dick. It's going to be a trial with a jury. The public defender will be working for Dick."

"Oh, really? His wife, Bette Robinson, is the person that leads the support group I go to. She and her partner describe themselves as 'addictive behavior specialists.' She's great."

"Well, I'm supposed to have a meeting with her before the trial starts. It begins next Tuesday at nine in the court annex."

"Is it open to other people? I'll go if you like."

"That would be great. Thank you for everything."

"I'm glad to do it. . . . It's really peaceful here, isn't it?"

"Yes. I needed this time. It's been so hectic and such a shock. This is peaceful. I needed it."

Some of the saddest times have a way of generating love. This was one of them.

Much time at the court hearing for Susan's boyfriend was given to Susan, and she again rose to the occasion. She was the only witness. It was a psychedelic time for her, in which each moment of that strange scenario was *unnaturally vivid*: Susan showing Rick the restraining order, Rick going up a step to the mobile home to talk to the police department, Dick coming out with the pistol and putting it no more than a foot from Rick's head—all this shrouded by the specter of Robin coming by, crazed and violent. Susan did not lose her composure or her lucidity. She had clearly known what she was doing and why: she had wanted her son to live in a healthier environment. I do not remember seeing Dick testify. Perhaps he did. I do know that he did not get first-degree murder. It was not premeditated. I do not remember what the verdict was. Perhaps it included some counseling. Susan did go to the therapist I

knew, the wife of the public defender. She told me Susan was frag-
ile; she was struck by Susan's vulnerability. I don't know much
about Susan's growing up, but nothing would surprise me. I
vaguely remember her saying she wasn't fond of her family—one
reason why she no longer lived in the mid-West. I relayed some of
this to Anthony, who was by then at Humboldt State. He didn't
really want to talk about it and didn't want to go to Rick's grave
when he was home on vacation.

IN 1990, AFTER I HAD MOVED BACK to Englewood to help my father, I received a letter from Susan, somewhere around Christmas
time, who was still at the trailer park in Carpenteria. The note included a snapshot of a little girl, Susan's granddaughter, Robin's
daughter. Susan was happy to care for the little girl. It gave her a
purpose she was happy to take. Another few years passed, and
again I heard from Susan. Another grandchild. Today her granddaughters would be in their late twenties. I wonder. We have not
been in touch for over ten years. I am tempted to write her. Might
she be caring for any great-grandchildren? Our worlds are so different. They had been before, but when we started as next-door neighbors with sons the same age, the gap didn't seem so wide. I wonder
if she is still alive, and if so, would I be glad, or would I regret looking her up in that single trailer car home in that mobile home park
in Carpenteria?

I'll think about that for a little while longer.

*Lawrence Francis Califano at the Botanical Gardens
in the Bronx, NY, 1962*

*Wedding reception March 2, 1963: Larry, Molly
and my aunt Elizabeth Folger Hazelton Boardman*

Natalie the Bride

*Grandma Molly Sweeney Califano
and Anthony Francis Califano, born March 27, 1967*

Larry wet-suiting it at Ledbetter Beach

Natalie Circa 1968; photo by Jason Lo Cicero

Jose

*Anthony's second birthday, March 1969,
with Larry, 410 ½ West Sola Street*

Anthony (on right) with his mischievous buddy, Paul Beyer, modeling clothes for a Brooks Photography student

Natalie plays the Clown in Punch & Judy

Frankie from Viet Nam, 1969

Circa 1974. Canastota, NY. Left to right: Lynn Beaumont, Anthony, Aunt Carol Szarcowicz Beaumont, Grandma Kay Beaumont, Lauren Beaumont

Circa 1974: Canastota, Lynn, Natalie, and Grandpa Butler Beaumont

Circa 1976: Natalie the ESL teacher in Kitchen at 410 ½ West Sola

Natalie (middle) in Marat-Sade *by Peter Weiss. Directed by Robert Weiss at the Santa Barbara Playhouse, circa 1976*

Poster of The Jewelled Heart,
Santa Barbara Playhouse/Plays for Children, circa 1977

The French Professor, Mark J. Temmer

Anthony, 1977

Anthony, 1978

Anthony the wrestler at 185 pounds, 1984
(chief executioner of the Guillotine).

Natalie house sitting by Pam and John Reynolds's pool

Anthony's graduation from San Marcos High School in Santa Barbara,
with his dad, Larry (right), and uncle Frankie (left), June, 1984

Natalie the torch singer, 1987

Natalie making her debut as a church soloist at the UU church
in Santa Barbara, singing "Pennies from Heaven" and
"Money Makes the World Go Round" from Cabaret

Natalie playing the part of a nun in the Opera Workshop's first production of Soeur Angelica, *directed by Elizabeth Layton. "See that your hearing and words are fraught with quiet and humble submission."*

BURNOUT

When you're behind on the rent, because
the paychecks you get from your morning job
as a teacher's aide don't cover the rent
as well as food and clothes
for your fourteen-year-old son
and nine-year-old daughter,

when your car breaks down;
when your son has to get eye tests costing $200.00,
when you quit your other job
as a waitress at Carrow's
because you can't get your studying done
and work nights, too,
when you lose a day of classes and study
because your daughter has head lice,

oh, and when your married boyfriend stops by,
unexpectedly,
on a Saturday night, in his new car,
on the way back from the car show,
and he tells you not to sleep around because of AIDS,
and he wants to get laid,
and you have a paper due next week,

when your ex-husband "forgets" to send
the child support,
even though he has a good job and the house,
and you don't want to get up in the morning,
that's burnout.

BURNOUT II

You're in grad school, paying four hundred a quarter,
while your pay check as a part-time instructor
doesn't cover the rent,
and you have no promise of full-time work,
even with the degree.
Your kid's grown out of his pants and shoes,
and now he needs thirty-five bucks
for his football uniform—
that on top of the fact that you just paid off
a thousand-dollar dental bill for a crown,
and now there's a nine-hundred-dollar repair
on the car.
Your boyfriend is flying to Germany.
He earns forty-five grand, and his company covers
almost all of his medical insurance.
Maybe once a month or so,
he feels expansive enough to take you
to a cheap chicken place for dinner;
otherwise, he's pretty liberated
and you go places Dutch.
He's concerned about your financial situation.
In fact, he's concerned about our relationship
on account of your financial situation.

So what have you got, in short?

(a) an insult;
(b) you're demoralized; but mostly
(c) you've got a lot of crap you just don't need.

THE JEWELED HEART
AND THE CARMEN DRESS

I N 1977 I WAS IN A CHILDREN'S PLAY called *The Jeweled Heart*. I played the leading role of a circus lady who becomes a princess. My son Anthony, then about ten, had a small part in it as well, and used to enjoy wrestling backstage with another boy his age. Bill Burkes was also in the cast; he played a boatman, and backstage he was making friends with Anthony, hoping to make friends with me.

Bill had dark, milky chocolate skin and green eyes set in a square, longish face. He was long-boned, about six feet tall, but not thin. He was a gentle person who spoke of having been raised on a ranch in Texas among whites and of adopting two sons, whom he had raised well. Bill's late father had been a tailor for Warner Brothers, and Bill, having been exposed to show biz, enjoyed his involvement in local theater, one being The Santa Barbara Playhouse—Plays for Children, which I was involved in.

One afternoon, towards the end of the run, he came up to me. "Natalie, I'm having a brunch a week from Sunday. Deb, Rick, and some other friends are coming. Would you come too, and help me host it?"

"Sure. Do you want me to bring something?"

"That'd be great—a coffee cake or something."

"I could make something. I just got a recipe for a pineapple walnut coffee cake. What time are you having it?"

"About ten. I'd like Anthony to come too, if he'd like."

"Where do you live?"

"On Cota Street, down past Gutierrez."

"Oh, that's easy. I'm not that far away."

"Great. I'll talk to you again about it next week."

Bill's friend Richard was also active in local theater, and they had been in some local productions together. Debra, Rick's live-in girlfriend, was an attractive blonde from the East Coast; I got to know both of them better when Bill and I started dating.

A fun-loving couple, they'd known Bill and his adopted sons for several years. Rich was about 5'10", of medium height, had salt-and pepper-hair, and could find humor in most things. Debra was fair-skinned and had almost platinum hair cut just above the shoulder, with bangs; her supportive husband encouraged her to attend Santa Barbara City College to get her AA degree. Though stylish, she was not vain. One Hallowe'en they stopped by on their way to a party. This couple stood at the door when I opened it: Rich had become a priest wearing the black-and-white clerical collar, and Deb had become a nun, wearing a habit that covered a very large abdomen. On a later Hallowe'en, Rich went as a sheik, and Deb was the spitting image of Marilyn Monroe. They have remained my friends for over thirty years. They look the same and have the same warmth and *joie de vivre* they had before. But I digress.

The pot-luck was very pleasant, and Anthony did stop by

briefly with his friend Rick Briggs, who lived up the street from Bill; they enjoyed the food, and I enjoyed their meeting my child-friendly friends.

After the brunch, I helped Bill clean up, and we sat and had a chat before I took off. The long, green, wood-framed couch extended along the wall before the entrance to the kitchen. It was a simple but neat, Sears-furnished one-bedroom apartment close to the hill below Santa Barbara City College, which overlooked the ocean. I lived maybe seven blocks away.

"Thanks for helping me. I enjoyed having you do it."

"Well, I had a nice time. I enjoyed meeting Debra and Rick," I said.

"I've known them for several years now. They're good friends. I've been in several Alhecama productions with Rick, and I really like the way Debra dresses. She's very attractive. My wife dressed really nicely, too."

"Oh? You were married?"

"Yes. She was a Polish princess."

"What happened to her?"

"She died in childbirth."

"You have a child?"

"Yes, a son."

"Where is he?"

"In Sweden, with my brother."

"What's your brother doing in Sweden?"

"He's a doctor."

Bill didn't offer but seemed to like being asked. I thought it interesting that he was so impressed with the way Debra dressed; I also wondered why his son would be raised by his brother while he was raising two adopted sons here.

It had been a nice time, though, and Bill asked if I'd like to do something the following weekend. He didn't specify what, but I wasn't dating anyone at the time, and he seemed nice enough, and I enjoyed Debra and Rick. It would be nice to do things with them and to get to know them better, as well as Bill.

The next weekend there was a party at the home of some friends of the three, so I joined them (a barbecue this time), and there was music and some dancing at one of those one-story, Goleta, ranch-style homes with a little grass in the front or back and a grill on the back patio. Most of the people were either married or had been dating for some time, and all seemed to know each other fairly well; most were from Bill's church, or from work.

Rick and Debra laughed a lot. On the dance floor they did a number impersonating free-style dancers moving with each other but apart, laughing all through it, Rick with his starting-to-gray hair, narrow face, and look of a middle-aged high school kid, and Debra with her fine, short blonde hair following the rest of her head as she and he swayed side to side, forward and back, mimicking with hilarity your cool, in, night-club groupies.

During one break I had a chance to talk to Debbie. "Bill really seems to value your friendship," I offered.

"Yes, friendship's very important to him, and Rick's gotten to know him quite well from 'Carousel' and a few other productions."

"How long's he been with the county?"

"Oh, about two years now. He got a masters in city planning from UCSB, I think with a student loan, and from there he went to this job."

"Well, it's not a bad job. He can travel to different areas in the county, which he enjoys. He gets benefits, which is a far cry from my job, and he seems to like the people."

"Yes, and he doesn't have to move, as Santa Barbara's such a central location in the county."

"Yeah. . . . Oh! He seems to be really impressed with the way you dress."

"Oh, yes. He has told me that on occasion."

"He also told me he'd been married to a Polish princess who died in childbirth, and how the child is in Sweden. That must have been a difficult time for him."

Debbie pursed her lips. "I'm not so sure about that one. We love Bill and appreciate the importance he places on friendship. He's a good person, but we really wonder about that particular story. He's not the most realistic guy around, that's for sure."

"I was wondering about that."

I wouldn't normally discuss such things with someone I had met only once before, but I suspected, correctly, that Deb and Rick were down-to-earth and unpretentious, so it was easy to bring up such things.

Shortly thereafter, Bill asked her to dance, and Rick asked me. I was glad that that group did not, as many groups do, dance with only one person.

Rick told me, in the course of the dance, that his brother Ron, a professional actor who had studied with Stella Adler, was one of those people who could talk in an extemporaneous monologue by the hour and keep people in stitches the whole time. That did not surprise me. Rick himself found humor in about anything and had a frequent, easily identifiable laugh that was the sound of hilarity itself.

I was not falling in love with Bill, but I enjoyed knowing him and his friends. However, I was not going to attempt to wear the same kind of clothing Deb wore; she was younger and shapely and didn't have a spare ounce on her. I wasn't heavy, but it just wouldn't be the same. I began to wonder if Bill needed to parent his girlfriends.

One morning I went to church with him, a Baptist church halfway between Santa Barbara and Goleta. The service was okay but hardly in the style of even a non-practicing Presbyterian. After church, we stopped by my apartment; when I got inside, I entered the kitchen and took some carrots out of the refrigerator. Bill came into the kitchen, too.

"Why are you avoiding me?" he asked in a tone that indicated he had figured something out.

"What are you talking about?"

"You walked right into the kitchen."

"Yes—I got some carrots. It's noon. Would you like one?"

"No, thank you." His voice always had a touch of Southern and British, and he sometimes forgot to add an "s" to the third-person singular in the present. As a white Anglo-Saxon versed in grammar all through school and now an English teacher, I couldn't help but notice. I liked dialects but had been speculating over how much of his was real, especially since he had already told me he wanted to "have no part of the black culture."

"You think I'm avoiding you because I went into the kitchen

and got some *carrots?"* This was irritating. What's his agenda? I wondered.

I didn't really get an answer to the question, but this and the suggestion that I should dress like Debra were causing me to clench my mental fists. It was only a matter of time before a verbal retort would follow. In any case, we had a sandwich and a cup of coffee and chatted a bit before he went off to call his sons and I started to correct some papers.

Later I got a call from Debra. "Hi, Debbie, how are you?"

"Fine. I just wanted to tell you that Rick got a call-back from La P'tit (Cabaret) for *Stalag 17,* and he told me that your brother-in-law got the lead."

"Oh, Frankie! That's *great.* That's quite a role. What's Rick going for?"

"I'm not sure. He read several parts. I think the one he'd like the most is the one who gets out of the barracks but then gets caught and killed."

"Keep me posted. It'll be great to see it, especially if there are a lot of people we know in it. . . . By the way, Debbie, I went to church with Bill today, and afterwards he seemed to assume that I was avoiding him because, when we got to my place, I went into the kitchen and took a carrot out of the icebox. It irritated me."

"Yeah, he has some funny ways."

"Between that and his telling me I should dress like you, I'm getting ready to let him know what I think of all that. What makes him think he's such a great dresser that he should give out all this advice?"

"Yeah, I know. Rick's said a few things to him on occasion, and he doesn't take offense, but I doubt it sinks in either."

"Well, it's just a matter of time before I say something." (I had inherited my mother's *modus operandi:* We will tolerate shit politely for so long, but when the saturation point is reached, you don't want to mess around with us further. It was also our way of rationalizing a weakness in assertiveness, but there you are.) I was getting ready to say something sooner rather than later. Of course by this time we had spent some nights together, and I was not entirely happy with his tendency of pouting at the idea of using a condom because of "losing some of the pleasure," even though I'd followed the advice of my good friend Alice, who suggested putting it on for him.

SOME SUNDAY AFTERNOONS LATER, Bill and I went to play volleyball and have a picnic on the Mesa above City College. We were playing on opposite sides. Bill slipped and twisted his knee. I turned toward him, but he gave me a look that said, "Don't make an issue of this." I stayed where I was; he sat down for awhile but then got up to play again. It was obviously hurting. Why would he do that? I thought. After the picnic, he took me home, and again—this time after playing a sweaty game like volleyball, said, "You know, you would look really great if you dressed more like Debbie."

"Bill, I am *not* Debbie, and her style is not *my* style. Who are *you* to tell me how I should dress? You don't have the greatest taste in clothing yourself. You don't even have the sense to stay off your knee when you've hurt it. Don't make decrees to me. I have one father. I don't need another. . . . Most people, by the way, think I dress just fine."

He didn't bring up the subject again. And his knee problem didn't go away. I was soon beginning to wonder why I was dating just this one person when I knew it wouldn't go anywhere. It wasn't the first time I'd gone through the motions of being in a one-on-one dating situation knowing the chances of "commitment" and "possibilities of a long-term relationship" weren't present.   Still, he was a good person, though I never knew whether he wanted just to date or something else. But maybe that is just as well.

One evening when I was supposed to go to a show with him, he stood me up and didn't call. The following morning, I took a walk down to his place, chewed him out, and told him that standing me up was unacceptable.

"I'm sorry," he apologized. "I went out with some buddies and neglected to pick up the phone." He was impressed that I would come over and chew him out, though.

What I had done the previous night, since I'd gotten tired of waiting for him, was to go up to La P'tit (Cabaret) to see a show. One of the characters in it, Raoul Navarro, had dated a friend of mine some years back, but in the intervening years had gotten into some trouble in local politics by supposedly bribing someone. The whole issue caused a mini-Watergate-type scandal, resulting in Raoul's year's visit to Chino.

He was a "chort Mehicano" but a talker, and charming. His father had gone blind from glaucoma and often smoked pot to relieve the pressure on the eyes. Raoul played a blind man very well in Catch-22, and he enjoyed smoking some pot when in the role (and out of it), a chip off the old block, as it were.

After the show, Raoul worked behind the bar, directly opposite the stage. He was shorter than I, with fine, dark, curly hair framing a round face; one eyelid was slightly more closed than the other, from an accident, I learned, that had caused partial blindness. He liked to laugh and talk to people.

"Are you the same Raoul Navarro that dated my good friend Maria Sotelo?" I asked when he was getting me a tequila sunrise.

He paused for a moment, as if taken off guard. "Yes, we were in love for awhile. She was a beautiful woman. But she had some self-destructive tendencies, too. Sometimes she called me at work when she'd been depressed and in bed all day and wanted me to come over right then and get in bed with her. I'd have to tell her, 'Honey, I can't get there right away, but I'll come when I finish here.'"

Well, I figured I wouldn't have to pump *this* guy for information.

"Yes, she had a hard life," I agreed, fiddling with the swizzle stick in my drink. "I helped her get her divorce. She was angry with God for a long time. Having been raised by two super-religious aunts and a self-serving, non-present father, then marrying someone who couldn't relate to her, and she was incredibly intelligent as well as being incredibly superstitious. . .well, as it turned out, she did remarry, and I sang in her wedding. We became very good friends."

I had a good time talking with Raoul, and I gave him my phone number. I told him I was dating Bill, but he must have known that I liked him some; he called during the week, opening the conversation with a raspy, "Is he there?" to let me know that he would be at La P'tit after the show the following weekend.

Bill and I went out on Friday, but on Saturday, being free, I went up there. Raoul seemed pleased to see me. I had been a little nervous about going, but my friend Alice had advised, "Oh, go on up! Raoul will know why you're there and be glad of it." Behind the bar, for a fleeting moment, he caught my eye, gave me a little bow, and continued drying a glass. Cute. When he was done, we had a drink (I the tequila sunrise, he a beer) and went next door to shoot a bit of pool—a new diversion for me, an old one for him. A former girlfriend of his appeared as we were leaving, and he brushed her off quickly and mentioned that he had dated her some time back. I wasn't threatened because I could tell he wasn't interested.

I knew I needed to do something, because I was more interested in spending time with Raoul. So on the advice of my shrink, Irwin, I called Bill and said I needed to talk to him. I went to his apartment, took his hand as instructed, and told him that I was not ready for a commitment with one person, that I had met Raoul and wanted to spend time with him.

Thanks to theater, they knew each other. Bill listened and handled it well. He asked me if it was because of his financial situation, as he had quite a few debts to pay and didn't handle money very well. I said no (although it could have been). He said that we should stay in touch and, as it was getting towards the Christmas holidays, he'd like to have me and Anthony for Christmas dinner, but Raoul could "have me for New Year's". Bill was quite religious. I said that would be okay.

Afterwards, I felt bad about the situation and the time of year, but was relieved that it was over and done.

That Christmas, though, was a fiasco for me. Typically, I was trying to please too many people. My ex, Larry, and his brother, Frank, traditionally came over on Christmas morning for coffee and danish, to bring Anthony some presents and be sociable, though they usually left in about a half hour. Anthony and I were going to Bill's for a noon dinner, and then, in the evening, the plan was that we would come home and cook a Christmas dinner with Raoul. Raoul had four children of his own and related to them well, and Anthony liked him. His wife was a Jehovah's Witness, but although they lived together, they had an "understanding" and were sure that eventually they would separate. For the present it was more convenient and cost effective to live separately under the same roof. By the Jehovah Witnesses, Raoul was considered one of the "worldly people."

As usual, Larry and Frank came and left in a half hour. Then Anthony went to hang out with a friend. By the time noon rolled around, he was nowhere to be found, so I went to Bill's by myself. Bill had made a lovely pot roast and had a box for me the shape of which indicated that the contents were clothing. I ate a light meal, knowing that I would be cooking some steak later. I opened the box and found a bright red sleeveless wrap-around dress on which large pink and red roses seemed to float, and, in spots, blue peacocks with bright green feathers. The wide neckline was low and round, and I had to admit he had picked a striking and sensual piece of clothing. I felt bad. The meal and the dress were an act of love. I did bring him a photo of Anthony and his friend Rick, now Bill's buddies, but that was easy, while he had gone out of his way to do something most considerate and very special. I was sorry I could not have stayed longer, but I was, as someone later described me, "running by the seat of my pants."

When I got home, there was still no Anthony. Raoul was due at 6:00 p.m. At about 5:45, Anthony wandered in to announce that he had already eaten. Raoul came at 6:00 and, seeing nothing ready for dinner, was unhappy. He got over it, but it wasn't the greatest way to begin a relationship, let alone end another. Let's just call it my worst Christmas.

I had a good time with Raoul in many ways. He liked to "wine and dine" the women in his life. He was working as a contractor and therefore made enough money to enjoy some spending. This was important to him. As a child, sometimes he had gone to elementary school without shoes.

Our first date was a trip to Cambria for the weekend, an artists' colony like Woodstock, New York. We drove north on Route 1, the scenic route—nice for me, since I always made the trip in a hurry on 101, to get to San Francisco or Sebastopol in the shortest time possible.

The road curved, and on that sunny but overcast Friday, I saw the crisp blue Pacific showcasing dots of small, mostly fishing, villages, around most of the bends.

Raoul liked to talk about the important things in his life, and there was time for that, too.

"When I went to Chino—and when we pass that spot, I will give it my usual greeting, a raised middle finger—my family had to go on welfare. But I was lucky afterwards to get a job through a friend working at the second-hand furniture store on Victoria

Street. I worked there for about eight years, you know? But I injured my back and had to stop. And then I got the job I have now, working with Gary. Gary's very ambition driven, I'd say, but he's doing well, and since I grew up in Santa Barbara, I know the area well, and a lot of people, and I can get in touch and talk to Spanish-speaking laborers if we need them. I'm like his right hand man, and I'm doing well. I'd like to write a book about my time in Chino and say what really happened. You're an English teacher. Wanna help me?"

"That sounds really interesting. I like to proofread. Have you started anything?"

"Well, I have a lot of letters and tapes—I'll show you later on. Anyway, Gary likes to party, sometimes even more than I want to, and I *always* like a good party. Once I took a date to a party, and I ran into my daughter Shelly with her date."

"And you're still married and living at home? Was that very awkward?"

"Oh, no. I said 'Hi,' and introduced her to my date. Well, my whole family understands the situation, and it's been that way for years. Eventually we'll get divorced, but Georgia and I have talked it through. She's committed to the Witnesses, and that's something I'm not interested in. I do like to go to mass on Christmas Eve. . .maybe you and Anthony will come with me, and then we could go out for a bite afterwards. . . . No, my kids understand, and we don't argue or anything at home. We're on good terms. We just have separate lives. Hers works for her, and mine works for me."

"Well, I'm glad to know that. When I was getting divorced, Larry and I *pretended* to be on good terms, but he was hurt and angry with me—that was obvious—and that just made it more difficult for me and Anthony. But we needed to *say* that we were on good terms. Mature and civilized. For the sake of our own egos, or something."

When we approached Cambria, the sky was more overcast, the air moist, almost drizzly, and once having reached our hotel, we strolled along, looking at tables set up to display small sculptures, some glass art, blown and painted, prints and etchings, silver items, all things one might see on a Sunday afternoon at the beach in Santa Barbara. Up there that day, the weather, without the bright Santa Barbara sun and the sharp contrast of bright colors, was almost like a drizzly day in New England.

We deposited our suitcases in the hotel and looked in craft shops, smoked a bit of pot, and went to dinner. I had smoked cigarettes some before, but not pot.

We sat at a small, square table covered with a blue-and-white checked tablecloth, with a covered candle and a small vase containing two carnations. We ordered soup. Raoul got up to use the men's room. I picked up the soup spoon and put it in the cup. Then I raised the spoon to my mouth.

My head was suddenly suspended on a long broomstick-like pole almost to the ceiling. It was quite difficult to handle a bowl of soup that way. I wondered if I could finish it without spilling it all over. My mouth was so far away from the table, and my hand, and to eat a whole dinner like that was going to be a serious challenge. When Raoul came back from the men's room, I explained this dilemma to him. He laughed.

"That don't make *no le hace*. That's the effect of the stuff. Never hurt to spill a little. They get paid to clean up here." It was a highly amusing evening and dinner. We watched TV afterwards and found everything hysterically funny, and I wanted to remember it all, but the next day the only thing I could remember was that it was hysterically funny. What a disappointment!

Sometimes Raoul would spend time with his work partner, Gary, at one of the local watering holes over some drinks, and sometimes he would arrive at my apartment late, although he would usually call to let me know. Gary, an overweight, wheelchair-bound control freak and, I thought, person of questionable honesty, was jealous of the idea that Raoul was "in love" with me, and I didn't appreciate the fact that Raoul sometimes didn't show up when he said he would. But he did like the fact that I was a singer and enjoyed taking me to piano bars where I could sing a melody or two. He did *not*, however, like the fact that Al Reese, the piano player at Tommy's Golden Cock, was a good-looking African American and a friend of mine. His comment when I spoke to Al before leaving Tommy's one night: "Just another woman waiting in line to talk to Al Reese."

In the meantime, because I did sing and perform on dinner shows and in retirement and convalescent homes, I had the perfect outfit thanks to Bill Burk's Christmas gift. I especially liked to wear it when singing "Habanera" or "Seguedilla" from *Carmen*. It was probably the best outfit I had for singing my French cabaret and torch songs. Although I was not in love with Bill, I appreciated his gift and his friendship, and friendship was something he valued. Further, he was nice to my son, and as a single mother I had known many men who didn't know or care squat about the responsibilities or concerns of a parent. Bill had a good heart.

Sometimes, when I visited Debra and Rich, Bill would be there, and there was no tension between us, though at one point he explained to our hosts, "Natalie and I have a thing going." I didn't know what this "thing" was supposed to be, but we all knew Bill was like that. One night after we had broken up, he asked Anthony down to spend the night, and Anthony went. However, the next morning Anthony got upset when Bill teased him about having a girlfriend (not true), so he came home, and Bill later called and apologized.

Sometime later, Bill decided to run for city council. He asked Deb to proofread his resumé and some of his brochure material. Besides not knowing much about city issues, he did not write grammatically; Deb tried to help him, but the upshot was that Bill did not present well during a League of Women Voters debate and might have gotten ten votes max on Election Day. Besides the knee that he hadn't taken care of, he still had financial issues. Finally, he had been diagnosed with diabetes, which he didn't manage. He eventually moved near Los Angeles, where his mother had a mobile home. She lived to be about a hundred, and Bill predeceased her. Rick, Deb, and I wrote her and kept up some correspondence with her. She often wrote how much she missed her son.

Back to the *chort Mehicano*: He wanted to write his book about his stay at Chino, and at parties with the theater types, including my brother-in-law Frank as well as his brother, my ex Larry, Deb, and Rick, he would tell those who cared to listen, "Nats and I are going to write my story on being at Chino. I have letters and tapes ready to roll." Or it might just be in a bar with Raoul's brother and his drinking pals, including Richard Nelson, producer of the Santa Barbara Playhouse, whom I had been head over heels in love with.

Raoul brought all his letters and tapes to my apartment. He started the opening paragraph something like:

The cop pressed the buzzer and opened the large metal door into a cavern-like gray hall where the sound of each footstep echoed through the morgue-like building; we heard the sound of our foot-steps rise and disappear. The door clanged closed behind us, and I was led to a hallway with bars on one side and a concrete wall on the other. There was an eerie quiet sitting in the air, as humidity sits, weighing you down, zapping your energy with a subduing, ominous lassitude.

In one corner of my living room, I had a pile of yellow note pads with scrawls on a couple, and the written-on sheets turned back; then there were cassette tapes in a bag, and a cassette player, neither used at all, and some letters. They remained there for about six months, unattended to by either of us except for an occasional perusal on my part, wondering whether Raoul thought that, through osmosis, all this material would enter my brain and I could just whip it out with my trusty manual typewriter.

I was beginning to notice some unsettling things about Raoul. There were times when, after imbibing a lot, some switch turned off in his brain and created a disconnect in his rational faculties. Not that he was violent; he was just weird. On one occasion, I told him to leave. On another, we were going to see a movie with a female friend of mine after having a light dinner at my place. Raoul didn't show up until it was time to leave, so my friend and I went, and Raoul, a bit loopy, crashed on my couch. When I got back at about 10:30 p.m., he woke up and walked to his home on the mesa, symbolically doing penance. And I saw some of what he called "being giving" as a form of manipulation. So I began to detach from him, which was a plus for his friend and controlling partner, Gary.

At one time when we were "in love," Raoul liked to think that we could communicate through silent thought-waves. I considered that to be bullshit, to put it bluntly. And on the tackier side, if I wasn't up for sex when he was horny, he let me know that he could find it elsewhere, to which I responded by saying, "Go right ahead."

The way I eventually broke up with him was by saying that, since he was still living with his wife, regardless of *their* relationship, I was not going to be committed to someone who lived with a partner. He assured me it could be worked out, but I was not willing to give up my independence to hang in.

Eventually he and his wife did get divorced, and they did remain on good terms, and Raoul was very proud of being fair-minded to his now-ex; I give him credit for that. But before all that happened, he dated the daughter of a theater friend. The girl was the same age as his daughter. As the worldly older man, he wined and dined her until she got restless and interested in guys her age who played music and smoked pot. Cynic as I had become, I saw through his pose as being that of the father figure with the way-ward daughter. That happens: The worldly older guy impresses the sweet young things, but then she gets independent and restless.

Some time after our breakup I ran into Raoul in a Mexican restaurant on Milpas (Cornfield) Street that had delicious fish tacos with black beans; he told me about the equitable divorce, that he was proud of it, and that he had a female friend and they weren't officially committed (whatever that means) but enjoyed going on trips together. Sounded good to me. . .why not?

RAPPED BY MARIJUANA OR SOMETHING

I N ABOUT 1976, I THINK, on a sunny day in sunny Santa Barbara, I began to work on a few songs for Singer's Showcase, an organization that gave singers an opportunity to prepare songs with an accompanist (at ten bucks an hour) to sing (for free) at retirement and convalescent homes. Kathy McDermott, then in her twenties, had been in music all her life; she sang and played piano, organ, and flute. She had studied with the same distinguished voice teacher I had, Mrs. Lura Dolas. I drove across town to East Pedregosa Street, to Kathy's, to go over my songs. At her little house, on a street lined with palm trees, we worked on "Habanera," "Someone to Watch Over Me," and "Besame Mucho." Kathy played a recording of "Habanera" from the Metropolitan Opera, with some famous opera singer, to help me with phrasing, musicality, and intonation. She also had fine, home-grown marijuana that she cultivated in her tiny back yard.

After our session, that hospitable soul, with jaw-length brown hair and squarish glasses shielding a set of blue eyes in a square face, cordially inquired, "Would you like to have a few hits, Natalie?"

I had smoked once or twice only, and the inhalation hurt my throat a little, but I thought, why not? So I said sure, and she, on her two sturdy, shortish legs, opened her kitchen door to the little yard and obtained from a sunny shelf enough dry weed to roll a cigarette.

She took a hit, and I took a hit, she and I, she and I, about five times. Suddenly, I felt as if I had been rapped on one side of my head, and something in my perception changed. I can't describe exactly what, but space seemed to fluctuate. Kathy's brown hair and square face came closer, then drifted farther away. The piano was over to the right, then farther back, a little more left. I thought I was going to black out a couple of times.

Kathy studied me. "Are you all right, Natalie?"

"I'm not sure," I replied distantly.

"Are you going to be able to drive home? Wait a little while, and then see how you feel."

"Okay," I said vaguely.

"What's going on?"

"Everything looks different. Things don't stay in the same place, and their shapes change." Actually, I was scared. I could tell when I got a little high on alcohol and knew to drink water if that happened, but I sure didn't know how to deal with this or what would happen next.

About fifteen minutes later, I said I thought I could drive home, and started out in my car. Had a policeman seen me driving to the west side, creeping along at about 10 mph, he probably would have stopped me for going too slowly, but I wouldn't have dared go any faster. A tree probably would have jumped right on my car.

I got home; then, when I was standing in my kitchen, the wall opposite me and my square brown kitchen table seemed to be moving forward and back.

The phone rang. It was Raoul. What a relief to hear his voice. He knew about these things.

"How's it going, Nat?"

"I feel really strange. I just smoked some pot with Kathy, and I feel odd. I don't know what to expect, and it's scary. Everything seems to be moving its position."

He chuckled. "Don't worry, Nat. Go lie down and have a nice dream. In about a half hour, it'll wear off, and you should be back to normal after that, or at least normal enough."

"Oh, thanks. I have to pick up Anthony's friend David at the bus at 5:30, and I was scared enough driving back here. I just crept along."

"You'll be okay. I'll call you later tonight and see how you're doing."

"Thanks, I needed that. I'll go take a nap." We hung up.

FIFTEEN MINUTES LATER, Anthony came home from school and checked out the refrigerator. "What's for dinner, Mom?"

"Salad with ranch dressing and hot dogs in tortillas. I got frozen yogurt for dessert. We can pick up David in about a half hour," I added from my bedroom.

Thirty minutes later, Anthony and I were in my blue Toyota, slowly driving around the corner onto Anapamu Street, then onto

Carrillo and under the freeway, two blocks to the bus station. We waited about fifteen minutes for the bus, and there was David, so the car crept back home and I fixed dinner.

The two ten-year-old boys started joking.

"Got some bennies?"

"No, I only used yellow jackets. Or maryjane."

I was still shaken by my recent experience. "Don't joke about that stuff," I said with passion. "It's dangerous! You never know what's in it or, how it's made, or whether it's strong or laced with something else. It's very dangerous. It killed a friend of your dad's."

I really got on a soap box.

I will never forget that first whap on the side of my head, causing most stationary things to move closer and farther away, that put me into an unknown and frightening realm of perception in 1976, thanks to a few hits of your homegrown weed.

My Fortieth Birthday

M
Y PARENTS FREQUENTLY USED the phrase "life begins at forty," and I always liked it. When I was
actually nearing that landmark, I was single. I
would have liked to throw a fortieth birthday party and invite every friend I had made since coming to Santa Barbara,
but since my two-bedroom apartment was too small to con-
tain all of them, I decided to pay for a space at Oak Park, up
Castillo Street just past Cottage Hospital, where there was
plenty of space and an easy, well-known landmark. I had
planned several of Anthony's birthday parties there.

My guest list was expansive: I invited Tom and Doris Mooney,
who were the first people I had met in Santa Barbara, other than
my cousins, and Pauline McPherson who worked on the tapestry
The Seven Fruits of the Bible with me. Some of my neighbors on San
Pascual; Kim and her mother in Apartment 8; the super, Wayne,
and his family next to me in Apartment 4; my former neighbor, Es-
peranza, and her husband Roberto, from Mexico; my music friends,
such as pianists Alice soon-to-be Bourland, Jean Olson, Mme. Elizabeth Layton from the opera workshop, Joan, my mezzo buddy,
Pat Richardson, soon to be married—and her fiancé; also invited:

several men in my life, such as Larry Califano, my ex, Dick Nelson and Mrs. Dolas, some of the theater department at Santa Barbara City College; Debra; Rick; and Bill Burkes (at this time, I had broken up with Bill and was dating Raoul). To keep things simple, I made it a pot-luck, which was the tradition for parties in general, and often even weddings, at that time and place.

I was quite excited because I wanted to make sure that certain of my friends met certain other friends whom I *knew* they would like—I even made some lists to make sure I remembered who should meet whom. And I made some salads and got enough paper plates and cups and plastic ware to make sure there were enough items for all my guests. It was from four until seven.

I arrived at Oak Park about an hour early and put out the tableware and my salads (my specialty then was salads, learned by watching my father years before, while hungrily leaning on the door to the pantry). People started to arrive. . .and arrive. . .and arrive. It was lovely seeing all of them from different parts of my life, sitting on picnic tables or lying on the grass, staying, hanging out unhurriedly. I walked around talking to one and all, and trying to remember who I wanted to meet whom. Alice (of course) noticed that I seemed to be wandering aimlessly, and as I passed by her, she said, "Natalie, sit down!" I did so, and looked around at everyone there who really seemed to be enjoying themselves. My concern over friends meeting friends was starting to give me a headache, so taking time to sit and regroup was helpful. I did note, though, that one person was not present: the man I was currently dating, Raoul!

When the party began to wind down, several people stayed to

help me clean up, and the two very last people to go were Mrs. Dolas and Dick Nelson. It was heartwarming to me. And a few days later when I asked Raoul what had happened that he hadn't come, he said that someone he knew had died. I didn't quite believe that.

CHRISTMAS

ONE CHRISTMAS I WENT to Mexico to visit a friend. On Christmas Eve, we took a twelve-hour bus ride from Mexico City to Huetamo, in Michoacán, where they speak with a sing-song accent, the men work in the fields, and the women cook everything from scratch. There, the division of labor had a real purpose: survival. When we got off the bus, about 7:00 a.m., we bought some deliciously fresh carrot juice after using a putrid ladies room and being harassed by a nasty, sleazy man who insisted on our paying him as if he were the owner of the stinking place. I was taller than he and would have loved to flatten him, but Maya advised against it. There were no cell phones there, but someone came to pick us up in a beat-up car and drove us about forty-five minutes to the home of Marcelo's parents out in the campo. Our hosts, the parents and sister of Marcelo, the husband of my friend and former student Maya, lived in a two-room adobe house — well, three if you count the porch, which served as a guest bedroom as well. You just put a sheet over the rope mattress, providing instant air conditioning! At night and in the morning, I listened to the snorting of the pigs, the ruffling of turkey feathers, the barking of the dogs, and the braying of the burros. For breakfast we had iguana soup with red powdered chili, corn tortillas made that morning (one of the ones I made had a hole in the middle of it, which Marcelo's sister picked up and announced, "Esto es hecho de Natalie"), and warm milk straight from the cow.

There was a large urn by the opening to the kitchen from which we could take rainwater to brush our teeth. If you needed a rest room, the men's was behind some bushes past the left side of the house—the women used it during the day when the men were working in the fields, and when they were at home, the women went behind some bushes past the back of the house. Sometimes there was real toilet paper; if not, leaves would do.

After breakfast, we took a two-hour hike; I, in my wrap-around halter dress, felt the warm sun on my back and prickles on my forehead from not having coffee in the morning.

We eventually reached the home of a cousin of Marcelo, ready to enjoy the cool inside of their house—or was it just a room? They had two little girls and a boy who had some reading books, so they were going to school someplace. But when they smiled, their teeth looked uncleaned and somewhat rotten; sugar cane was the most likely culprit. I hoped that they were the baby teeth.

Lunch was lovely: huge papayas, taken from the trees right there with a large clipper on a pole, which they would catch as they fell. I didn't understand all the Spanish, but Maya was a great interpreter and obviously felt comfortable with all these people, though they were quite different from her own Italian-Swiss forebears. Afterward, we took the hike back to our lodgings; it had cooled some, but I was happy to get a bit of sunburn, since it had been quite chilly when I left Santa Barbara and still was when I returned home.

Here, though, it was Christmas. The neighbors came by and shared flour tortillas dipped in a warm brown sugar syrup, and then we joined them going to the homes of other neighbors and sharing the sweet beverage.

That was all. It was simple; it was peaceful.

ANOTHER CHRISTMAS DAY

I WENT NOWHERE, SINCE I WAS SICK with colitis, spending
the day on the couch of my two-bedroom apartment,
helping my seven-year-old son play with his toys. It
was blessed but in a different way. Normally I was too busy
and too stressed to spend good time just being with my son,
and his dad, my ex, wasn't attentive in those days, though
he and his brother usually stopped by in the morning for
coffee and sweet rolls. We had the rest of the day to hang
out and have a nice meal—not turkey, but probably steak,
broccoli, and salad with ice-cream for Anthony (colitis limited my diet). Two part-time jobs didn't bring in big bucks,
and my dedicated volunteering at a community theatre was-
n't lucrative either. In short, I was shot: tired and grouchy.
But that Christmas, I cherished spending the whole day with
Anthony. I helped him put together his toys and played
with him. I still remember how good it felt just to be there
relaxing—no appointments, no assignments, simply sharing
a day with my kid. Alas, sometimes it takes getting sick to
do the things we should be doing for ourselves and for those
we love.

I went far to find peace; I stayed home to find joy, and I remember what Blake said: "Christ spoke in parables to the blind."

THE CROW

When walking,
the crow resembles a rocking chair in slow motion.
He leans forward, tilts his head to one side,
leans back, then forth again,
then tilts his head to the other.

Sometimes he pauses,
tilts his head to both sides, slo mo,
takes another pause,
caws loudly.

That's how James Ashley did it
in the Santa Barbara Playhouse version
of Reynard the Fox.

We did a scene from the show
at a summer day camp, for publicity.
On the way home,
we stopped by the El Paseo
for something cold to drink.
We figured people sitting at outside tables
would enjoy hobnobbing with a few animals.

James notices that the side door
to the restaurant is open.
He goes in and, crow style,
starts up some stairs to an upper balcony.
It gets quiet in the restaurant
as the diners stop eating and observe
this human-style crow
stalk up the stairs.

James pauses, leans forward,
looks across the large room
into the scowling face of the proprietor.

For a very long minute,
James is dead still.
Suddenly he caws like hell,
then flurries down the stairs and out the door.

FRAN THE COSTUME LADY

Fran's died; I feel the same as when she lived —
gratitude and joy for knowing her.

Her life was costumes, grandkids, stories, jokes.
She liked her bourbon, and she liked her smokes.

They countered all the cortisone she took
for her arthritis — she ignored it, though.

Harried, worn down, I'd walk to Fran's and chat.
She'd tell me of her sons, her men, her shrink

who crossed the line from help to violation.
Her gay men friends were safer — had no strings.

Leaving Fran's,
I thought that those hard times would pass.
They did, and thank you, Fran, for peace of mind.

ELLIOTT SCHAFNER NELSON NEWMAN

When Elliott died, I was sad.
I'll tell you why:
Her life was sad.

She was intelligent, beautiful, wealthy.
Her mother died; her manic-depressive father
remarried, and she, also manic-depressive,
became a Cinderella.

She tried to kill herself once or twice;
She went to a shrink, who told her
she wanted to be a man
because she liked wearing pants!

When she married Richard Nelson, a man of good
peasant stock, her father said, "Good for the genes."
They had a daughter, Meaghan.

Elliott left Dick, though, and married the Neuman guy;
Then she left him and moved to Santa Barbara,
Where her father and stepmother lived.

But she was drinking, and her housekeeper,

worried for the child's safety,
called Dick in Tucson, where he was working
in the Theater Department at the U. of T.

Dick rejoined Elliott for the sake of the child
and to build their dream:
to start a community theater, including
a children's theater where no child
was excluded for lack of funds.

Still bipolar, Elliott went on drinking;
one day found her out cold
on the living room floor.

She went to the ER,
was admitted, got medication,
which helped, and she began acting again,
which was her first love.

Dick did a bit of drinking too,
and considered himself single; she didn't care.
She wasn't interested in sex.
Meaghan adored her father.

Dick got engaged to a woman.
They took Elliott to dinner on her birthday
and gave her the news.
She was no little bit ticked.

But Dick got drunk and behaved badly,
so the fiancée kicked him out.
He asked Elliott if he could come back.
She said no and moved back to Tucson
where she adopted a menagerie of animals.

She'd call long distance and talk for hours
while the animals made a mess.
She'd developed a cyst on her brain.
"No one's going to mess with my head,"
she said.

So it took its course.

Rachel Ward

British.
Short, elderly,
she taught pronunciation and radio
in the old country,
and wrote some songs when in a piano class
that she played for me once.

At Santa Barbara City College, in ESL, she taught
vocabulary and pronunciation through singing.
She had written and published a book
on pronunciation,
meticulously done.

Rachel made lemon curd occasionally
and cookies that weren't too sweet.

Then she was switched from teaching ESL
to working with students in the Writing Lab.
As she became engrossed in the students' papers,
leaning on her elbow,
she inadvertently elbowed the books
on to the floor
unless I caught them first.

The head of the Writing Lab
decided not to rehire Rachel,
so she came in to work anyway as a volunteer,
since she wanted to stay active,
and she was always interested in her students.
She was also lonely—she had no family here.

Then one day she didn't come in.
Someone phoned her, but there was no answer.
I was out of town, but a friend wrote me.
She had quietly left us.

NIGHTMARE

The soldiers,
with their green pants and helmets and guns,
were chasing me again.

I never knew why they were after me,
but they were, all too often.
I had to get away from them: easy—fly!

I could fly high over the trees
and over the roof of the family house.
I could land in the trees or on the roof,
and they couldn't get at me.

Once they tried when I was inside.
I got up to the ceiling of a bedroom
and then flew over their heads
as they came up the stairs.
I got out just in time—
I was beginning to feel trapped in there.

Again and again they came after me.
Once one of them tried to get me on the stairs,
but I fought him and got away.

For awhile, the soldiers stopped chasing me.
But then, just last night,
there was another one.
I was on top of a roof,
then on top of a bunk bed,
and this one kept talking to me;

in fact, we had a running dialogue.

All the time we were talking,
I was throwing pillows and blankets and quilts
down on him to keep him away.
He was big and heavy-set, with a round face.

What the hell do these soldiers want of me?
I didn't do anything to them,
And I'm tired of flying.

Peter Nelson, Psychic

I DON'T MAKE ANY SENSE out of this at all," says Peter Nelson, the psychic, lowering my watch from his forehead, where he has held it for about five minutes. "I'm lying under a train that whizzes along. I can't raise my head or an arm, or it will be clipped off. But the train passes and a strawberry blond gets up and walks away."

'That's how I feel," I comment. "I'm working part time and have been raising a son alone for fifteen years. I have financial pressures, and I'm in my second year of graduate school, have gained twenty pounds, and it feels as if it will never end."

"Well, that makes sense," Peter replies. "I also see someone walking along the streets of New York, looking at all the faces. I always do that, but you are one of the few people who does it as well. And I see a connection with death there."

"When I was a medical social worker in New York, I had one cancer patient I felt as if I had abandoned. She was a beautiful, dark-skinned Puerto Rican woman with green eyes who died shortly after I left for California."

"There's an issue there that needs to be looked at. You need to face it, as it is an undermining force. In order to become fully creative and fulfilled, you need to go back and understand it. Perhaps the woman who died was a symbol for something else that has been unresolved."

I leave Peter's office feeling as if a burden has been lifted from my shoulders. A therapist makes you do all the work, but this psychic's description of what he saw and reflected was just as helpful, if not more so. I've been feeling stuck, as if my life were on hold. Now I realize that this trek will end in a year and I can get on with my life. Seeing him was a well-chosen Christmas present to myself.

I happened to mention my visit to Peter Nelson in a letter to my parents—that I had heard his lecture (*a psychic!*)—and my father was alarmed. I was in California, where people, in his dim view, are "vegetarians or religious fanatics." He sent me several issues of the *Skeptical Enquirer.*

My father took great pride in being skeptical, which I thought was good, but that didn't stop me from looking into what psychics do. One friend I knew had studied both the psychic world and the skeptical world. He said that our psychic abilities are not so unnatural. Consider a conversation you are having with a friend. You are engrossed in that conversation. But your subconscious picks up that the person has circles under his eyes, is talking slowly, and looks pale. Later, you realize this and ask him if he is okay. In short, we can pick up clues even when we aren't paying strict attention to them.

So I don't know how Peter Nelson figured out, when he held my watch to his forehead for several minutes, how he *got* the image, but it was pretty accurate, *symbolically*: That word is suspect too according to my good father, E.B.B.

Peter Nelson lived in Australia. But he toured in many places of the world. Ironically, it was the world of science and medicine that brought him to his current career. In his lecture, he explained that he had been in medical school, in a lab doing monkey experiments, when, on a break, someone showed him a photo in a magazine of a countryside in England, whereupon he walked out of the lab, packed some clothes, and took a plane to England. He located a place that taught about the supernatural and entered the classroom. The lecturer saw him and said, "Hello, Peter—you're not expected here, but someone is waiting for you at another place." He went to the other place, and a woman, who became his mentor, was indeed expecting him—don't ask me, that's the way *he* told it. I plead ignorance, although some of what is deemed "psychic" seems believable, to me.

Call it insight, or intuition, and don't believe what sounds far-fetched. I learned from my father how important words are. The trick is to put the concept in a language that the person can relate to. If it's put in a dogmatic or hocus-pocus way, it won't fly with a lot of people. And a good thing, too, Dad.

REVEREND FOOARD

R EV. FOOARD WAS A SPIRITUALIST. At 6:00 p.m. on Friday evenings, you could go into a small, unobtrusive church on Santa Barbara Street, write two questions on a small piece of paper, pay five dollars, get a bite to eat at a funky restaurant a block away, and come back to the 7:00 p.m. session. People's questions were taken on a first-come, first-served basis.

The first time I went, it was with my two singing buddies, Pat and Joan. Joan wanted to know if her rocky marriage would last. I wanted a sense of direction, since my job as a part-time instructor at the local community college was becoming increasingly frustrating. Pat had some financial concerns, thanks to her flighty musician husband.

Pat drove us to the place, since she'd been there before. Leave it to her to find something interesting and a bit off the beaten track. We went into the old, dark, musty building, wrote down our questions, folded the papers, and clipped them onto a board, then moseyed down to the Sojourner's Restaurant for a light, inexpensive repast: a large chunk of cornbread and salad for Pat, rice and beans topped with grated cheese for me, and a tuna melt for Joan, along with peach-flavored iced tea.

Sitting at the wide window and looking out the still-bright day at the reconstruction of the Presidio, Pat reminded us, "He won't answer specific questions about what will actually happen in the future, but he *will* tell you about people you know who have passed over. I want to know about my aunt, who died five years ago. I really miss her. You know, my mother is in Disneyland most of the time."

Pat, the artist, divorced with two kids, took a bite of her cornbread and let the crumbs fall on to her salad. Her large, brown eyes expressing creativity, *joie de vivre*, and a strong preference for a man in her life. She was feeling that a curly perm for her shoulder-length brown hair would be most attractive, and it was certainly something different.

Joan, five foot two, a bookkeeper for Pueblo Radiology who watched pennies so she could spend them on trips and generous gifts for her children, was highly frustrated with her husband's indifference—make that obliviousness—to financial stability, though there was no doubt of their mutual love.

"Well, I really don't know what I am going to do," Joan began. "Dale didn't tell me before we were married that he was virtually bankrupt, and I don't want to pay off all his debts when he's just piddling in real estate and never makes any sales. He gets defensive when I make remarks, but what's he think I'm supposed to do? Not to mention his son, who's flunking out of school, and his ex-wife, who just lets him do it and makes no demands on him except to take up Dale's time with her bitching." Joan, not at all tall, had a short brown bob and a rich mezzo voice that could fill a room;

she told me when *my* songs—I'm also a mezzo—were too high for me. In response, I told her to try to pronounce her final consonants. I teach ESL. I know about that.

Soon enough, 6:50 p.m. rolled around—time to go. We paid and made our way back up the block in the bright sunlight on Santa Barbara Street, lined with palm trees, to the little old wooden church.

When we got there at 7:00, someone was playing an old piano. We sat down towards the front and looked around at three other groups of two or three people. There were no stained-glass windows, just a table for an altar; the faded, flowered wallpaper made it drab but homey.

Five minutes later, Rev. Fooard came through a door in front of us; he sat down and introduced himself by saying that he was a spiritualist, and was anyone scared? No one nodded, raised a hand, or spoke—guess not.

He was a man in his eighties, probably, lean and of medium stature, with a gentle demeanor, and he exuded an air of dignity, enhanced by the trace of a British accent. His age and appearance in that small, old church gave a feeling of the compatibility you taste in wine aged in the same skin, a slightly musty odor, but comfortable and friendly.

Rev. Fooard said there was nothing to *be* afraid of, for when he talked to those who had "passed over" it was done with love, and that he was not a predictor of doom. Then he took the first sheet of questions, held it in his hand, and asked to hear that person's voice. Still without reading, he would speak, usually with his eyes closed.

When it was my turn, he started the same way:

"There are some relatives looking over you, and they send a lot of love," he began. "One of them was an engineer of some kind and is giving you a tool. Who would that be?"

I was surprised to think right away of my grandfather, whom I never knew, since he died before I was born. "I guess my grandfather!"

"Well, he's giving you one of those tools you use to measure whether a building is straight or crooked, seeing as your life has been rather up and down. This tool will help you stay on an even keel."

How true! I was amazed and amused, as were Pat and Joan. We chuckled.

"Well," the Reverend went on, "it seems that you are being used—but that's not so bad. At least you have something to *be* used—a gift, or an ability. Is there something that concerns you about that?"

"I'm getting tired of being exploited by my job," I said. "I thought of changing jobs and working for the post office, but I don't really want to do that."

"It will shift at some point, if you stay with it a little longer." I had almost moved to Chicago to live with an old boyfriend, but he'd turned out to be an alcoholic and wasn't ready to leave his wife, so it was comforting to have someone tell me to stay put for awhile.

"Now I see a microphone—does that mean anything to you?"

"Yes," I said. "I like to sing." I was also wondering whether I should break up with my boyfriend, but it wasn't one of the questions.

"Oh, yes, that would make sense. Well, there is some part of you that will make a decision and not waver in that no matter what—for better or for worse." Perhaps I was more like my grandmother than I realized. Time would have to answer *that* question.

"Something happened to shatter you when you were young, but you're putting the pieces back together and you're going to be all right. There's plenty of people on the other side sending love." That was his last gem. I remembered the first time I saw my mother drunk, and of all the relatives I knew about who had died before I arrived.

Joan, after a resonant, "Good evening, Reverend Fooard," *did* get some love and support from her forebears on the other side; she and her husband had an interesting journey but remained more together than separate. About a year later, she moved to Visalia to be near her daughter, son-in-law, and two grandsons; she bought a house, saved pennies to buy gifts for her grandsons. About a year after that, Dale straightened out his finances as best he could, joined her, and spent some time in real estate—didn't make a lot of sales, but didn't get into debt either.

Pat received love from her aunt on the other side and got into the master's education program at UCSB; she didn't finish but taught some art and was inappropriately placed in history and English classes at a Catholic high school. She remarried but husband number three was abusive, so it didn't last.

When we left that little church and our time with the reverend, I felt as if I were Cinderella, and my fairy godmother—or was it my grandmother—had just made something a whole lot better with her magic wand and sent me on my way.

And some years later, when I moved back to the house I grew up in, I found that plumb line in my great-grandfather's (and later my father's) workroom in the cellar!

Joan remains in Visalia, but Pat, after splitting with husband number three, drove east with her son and a friend of his. She took them to Washington D.C. and then phoned me: "Natalie, I'm coming east. You need me to visit you!" She spent a week with me. We went to the Statue of Liberty and into New York with the boys. I was glad she'd come. The day after she left, I was on the bus, going into New York through the Lincoln Tunnel, when I had a strange fear that I was going to die. Two days later, I got a call from Pat's brother in Santa Barbara. Pat had been killed in a car crash on the way home. The two boys had been injured but were in stable condition. Her son and his sister went to live with her brother. Rev. Fooard, sadly, died of cancer a few years after our visits. Does anybody know of any good spiritualists? I have a few more friends and relatives on the other side now.

Editor,
Santa Barbara News-Press
P.O. Box 1359
Santa Barbara, CA 93102

October 16, 1994

I recently read the letter, published on September 24, by UCSB Economics Professor Robert Carrington-Crouch, who refers to Mindy Lorenz as an academic "gypsy" because she is a part-time lecturer at California State University, Northridge and Ventura. He says she is being economical with the "truth" because she refers to herself as a professor.

As a professor of Economics, Mr. Carrington-Crouch knows that colleges and universities hire many part-time instructors as a matter of economic convenience; they do not have to pay these people benefits, and without them, the universities would be seriously limited in what they could offer. To say that part-time instructors are "the exact opposite end of the academic scale to professor" says nothing. Scale of *what*, Mr. Carrington-Crouch? Does that include the ones who graduated from UCSB?

Many part-time instructors are professionals on a par or better than tenured professors, and they are obviously not in it for the money! Mr. Carrington-Crouch's line of thinking is the kind that white men used to devastate the Indian population of this country in the 1800's because they were "savages," and that justified murder, or with African Americans, slavery: Don't teach them to read; therefore they are ignorant and only fit to be slaves.

In closing his letter, Mr. Carrington-Crouch suggests that Lorenz and her supporters speak the whole truth and nothing but." I suggest that Mr. Carrington-Crouch do the same.

Natalie Beaumont
Englewood, New Jersey

THE ADVENTURES
AND CULTURAL HABITS
OF MR. VENTURA DE DIOS

THERE WERE TIMES WHEN I was teaching Adult Education English as a Second Language two nights a week that I had to find a baby sitter at the last minute. And sometimes it caused me to run a little late. I would hurry into my elementary school classroom with the childrens' tables and desks and would see Mr. De Dios, tongue in cheek, looking at his watch. When he and other paysanos came in late, they would greet everyone in the classroom—no matter that I was in the middle of teaching some point from the level-three book I was using. Since Mr. De Dios had been in Santa Barbara for a good many years, he spoke well, though writing and grammar were not his strong points.

I admired him. He was a good husband and father and had become a foreman on his job; in short, he was a decent, trustworthy man with a good sense of humor.

On one occasion, Mr. De Dios was having a party and invited me and my husband. I told him that, being divorced, I didn't have one. He apologized but said it would not be correct to invite me as a single woman. He was not judgmental; he simply expressed what was appropriate for that kind of setting. He was making sure that neither I nor his guests (wives and husbands) would be in an awkward position. This was in the late '60s and early '70s; the Hispanic culture in California had not caught up with the evolving Anglo culture.

In fact, on one Tuesday or Thursday night, I had only four students in my class, all male. One student asked why the rate of divorce was so high in the United States.

I thought of all the reasons I could: People get married before they really know what they want and are not prepared for the responsibilities; more women are self-supporting and don't need to marry for economic reasons; their perspectives and interests change; people live longer; more people admit they are not happy in their marriages; women are less tolerant of adultery and/or feel it gives them license to do the same.

And I also told them about a family I knew where the parents stayed together for the sake of the children. But the negativity the children grew up with had a very devastating effect on them and nearly destroyed the youngest emotionally.

Finally one of the men asked me if I was divorced. I told them I was. Within two weeks, none of those four men showed up in my class again. I wasn't really offended. It simply confirmed what I was already aware of: Divorce in some cultures is still as taboo as it was when I was growing up. Mr. De Dios was an open-minded, decent man.

CALIFORNIA SERVING STYLES

At the beginning of each Adult Education school year, I often had a get-together pot-luck in my two-bedroom apartment. It gave me an opportunity to catch up with former students and to find out who would be continuing with me. I didn't have a lot of space but could put the main dishes on a square folding table in the living room, and the desserts on a round unfinished table that I had sanded and shellacked myself; the drinks would be on the counter in the kitchen. At the time, Anthony was seven or eight years old.

On the appointed evening, my students would arrive: Chinese, Argentinian, Brazilian, Mexican, Japanese, Korean, French, Swedish, and with them an array of prepared and delectable foods. California style, I had the plates and on one side of the table and asked them to help themselves.

No one got up.

"Who would like to start?" I asked, looking for the one who would be more assertive in this situation.

No one got up. There was a pause. Then Mr. Dios got up and started filling a plate and handing it to the nearest student. He filled another plate, which Anthony gave to another student. They continued serving our guests.

"Mrs. Califano, you are supposed to serve your guests," said Mr. De Dios.

"This is California," I replied. "It's okay to help yourself." I think they got it but weren't ready to try it. Anyway, I loved the idea of Mr. De Dios and Anthony making a hospitality team!

SALIDO DE DIOS

Mr. De Dios had a brother living in Mexico who was interested in coming north to find work (and hopefully a green card) and to send money to his woman and their nine or so children. As we were chatting after class one day, Mr. De Dios asked me if I would consider having a marriage of convenience so his brother could come here legally. He offered me a thousand dollars. He said it would be strictly on the up and up, and I believed him. I asked him, "Well, if you are Ventura, is your brother Salido?" (I thought it was a good question!)

I gave the idea some thought. It would be nice to have an extra thou for mad money, as I did not make much as a part-time ESL teacher. A friend of mine who also taught ESL had gotten married and was in the process of getting the marriage annulled now that the "husband" had his green card, but she thought the whole process was more trouble than it was worth.

Of course she might have had different guidelines than those Mr. De Dios was proposing, which were strictly business. I mentioned the idea to my sister, who was completely against it, as was another man in the Santa Barbara community. There were risks involved, of course, which would penalize both parties, sending one back across the border and imposing a large fine on the citizen.

Mr. De Dios's brother did come to Santa Barbara, but I declined the offer. Class ended for the summer, but when we started up in the fall, I asked Mr. De Dios how his brother was doing.

"Well, he went back to Mexico," he explained. "All the time he was here, the lady he was living with in Mexico never contacted him. So he decided to go back."

"Oh, I see. I guess it's just as well I didn't marry him. *Salido salió.*"

KANDO KOBAYASHI

Kando Kobayashi was a student in my Santa Barbara Adult Education ESL class in the late 1970s. He was a tall for a Japanese, handsome, bright, agreeable, and a very good student. He was a graduate student at the University of California at Santa Barbara's School of Environmental Studies. He spoke well, and he wrote well.

At the close of the winter quarter, I took my students to dinner at a Mexican restaurant owned by the husband of a student in a different class. Observing them in an environment other than that of the classroom brought out some interesting features in their outlook and behaviors.

All of my students, except for the Mexicans, ordered from the menu: *chile relleno, burritos, arroz con pollo, enchiladas,* the usual items to be seen in a Mexican restaurant. What did the Mexicans order? Beer. "Aren't you ordering anything for dinner?" I asked.

"No," they replied. "This restaurant is for tourists. We eat better food at home." Understandable, I thought, and that restaurant was geared to tourists, rather than some others that catered to the genuine Mexican palate.

Another student, a Korean, learned the word "Hi" around and about. Every time he wanted my attention, he would say, "Hi, Mrs. Natalie," to the point of overkill. I clarified the use of that greeting.

The most surprising difference in behavior came from Kando. He was acting like a standup comedian. He made jokes, he made puns, and his humor was quirky and off the wall. Finally I asked him, "Kando, you are so *different* here than you are in class! How come?"

He answered, with a smile, "In class, I am serious. At party, I am crazy!"

"Is this usual in Japan?"

"Yes, it is usual."

"And is this okay with wives? And are they like that also?"

"No, wives do not come."

"They don't? What do they do for *their* social life?"

"Sometimes they visit with their parents, or their sisters, or their friends."

"Oh, that doesn't seem fair, where the husbands go out and have a good time and the wives don't have the same freedom. That reminds me—what about geishas? Are they still in business?"

"Yes, geishas help, because the men work very long hours. They go to the geishas, and they can relax, have a massage, have some kind of drink. When they come home they are more relaxed and don't get angry with their wife or children."

"And the wives don't mind? Do they still have sex with geishas? I would feel as if something were wrong with me if my husband needed to have sex elsewhere."

"Not all geishas give sex. Some give tea and a massage."

"Yes, but is it really okay with the wives? If the men work twelve hours and then spend more time out, it doesn't leave much time for their families."

"They spend time with their families on the weekends and also on vacation."

Mrs. Ling, from China, was listening carefully to this conversation and shaking her head a great deal. She was not pleased, nor were some of the younger Asian women.

"I don't want to stay home and just have children," a younger, very pretty Chinese woman remarked. "I want a career. I want to be a veterinarian and support myself. It's not fair the men have all the opportunities."

"Yes, life is changing now," said Kando, unruffled. "That is okay."

The restaurant was quiet that Thursday evening, and we stayed and talked until about 9:30. I thought about the place. A student's husband also worked long hours, being the manager of at least four restaurants in the vicinity. He, too, though not Japanese, got some rest and relaxation outside the home. She also spent time with her parents and her friends. It was common knowledge that her husband fooled around. She had a look of loss in her demeanor. Later they divorced.

Another topic that arose that evening was the custom of the Japanese tea ceremony. Kando offered, "My wife knows how to prepare and perform a ceremony. She can prepare a tea ceremony for the class."

And she did, at my apartment at 4:00 p.m. on a Saturday afternoon. All the students who were able came. Those of us who could sat on my unattractive brown and yellow wall-to-wall shag carpeting, around a square cloth where the authentic green-tea powder and the cups were placed. His wife, also tall, attractive, and gracious, quietly went through the correct motions in her preparation and actual service of the tea. Although I don't remember all of them, one was a circular motion with her arm above the container of the steeping tea in the water. My futon couch and square table with the Formica top, and my TV, were all pushed close to the wall, so we had enough space in the center of the room, and I arranged chairs around the cloth for those who needed them. It was quiet, with only Kando explaining what the motions meant. There was just the quiet and the unique flavor of the green tea with no sugar, salt, or anything else to munch on. By five-thirty, the ceremony was over, and my students left, thanking Kando and his wife for creating such a surprising peaceful atmosphere. When they had all gone, I noticed how relaxed and energized I had become. How amazing, I thought, that there are so many practical customs and practices in other countries that we in this country can benefit from. And that is one reason why I love teaching ESL

Fortunately, grammar came easy to me. But to do that and get back so much in return about people, their lives, and customs — well, I couldn't afford to travel a lot then, but I had the world in my classroom.

I still have a souvenir that I received from Kando before he returned to Japan. It's a long, black silk jacket with Japanese characters on the back.

"What does it mean?" I asked him after opening it.

"It means 'Japanese Fire Department.'"

Sometimes new thoughts and ideas come when and where you least expect them! And I actually wore the jacket a few times and enjoyed translating the characters on the back.

Anthony Francis Califano (1)

D R. Frances Dorwin, when she noticed the shape of my abdomen, told me, "You're carrying your baby high. You'll have a boy, and he'll be on the small side." The prophecy was correct.

They say that, when one is pregnant, what is done before birth will have an impact on your baby. I didn't think of playing a lot of music during that time, but I walked a lot. I walked to work at St. Francis Hospital, and I took the long route home, i.e., down Salsipuedes (Get Out If You Can) Street, then along Cabrillo Boulevard and the beach area, then up Castillo Street until I reached Sola-—perhaps two or three miles. Emotionally, that time was therapeutic, but it also kept me in good shape, and Anthony became dedicated to sports—a very good thing.

Most parents can tell stories about their precious ones, and I will mention a few of the more memorable ones, starting with his baptism. Since at the time I was a non-practicing Presbyterian and Larry was a non-Catholic, we thought it best to have Anthony baptized privately by the Presbyterian minister. When making the appointment, I mentioned to him that I would like to talk about something else—the lack of communication in our marriage—but I didn't feel comfortable about it and so did not.

In any case, Anthony was baptized in the Presbyterian Church. About a year and a half later, Larry's mother, Mary (Molly) Sweeney came to visit, and her old friend, May Sugrue, had already moved here. They thought that Anthony should be baptized in the Catholic Church, so, unbeknownst to me, while I was at work, they "kidnapped" Anthony and had him baptized in the Catholic Church.

I didn't learn about this until Anthony was a senior in high school, when Larry told me that, while he was at work back then, he'd gotten a frantic call from Brother Frankie saying, "Larry! Call the police! May and Molly are putting Anthony in a cab and taking him to the airport, back to New York!"

Had I known at the time that they had had the audacity to give my son a second baptism, I would have gotten angry, but after sixteen years, I thought it was amusing, and it was the story Anthony told when the seniors had to tell one story about themselves when little.

It was fortunate that I had a boy and not a girl, as at that time I was not into finding cute little matching outfits that also matched socks, purses, hats, coats, and all things princess, ballerina, or fairy. Once in a while I objected when Anthony wore a favorite shirt until it was threadbare, but usually clothing did not get much notice, except when Anthony was in high school and didn't ask his friends over when I wore a certain pair of pants that he hated.

Anthony did have blonde, curly hair when little. Since this was during the hippie era, one day I decided to put brown make-up on my face, and a blue shawl over my head, and put Anthony on my lap, a naked blonde, white baby, and have a friend take our picture, then send as cards with the caption, "Make love, not war." The photo didn't come out well, unfortunately.

Anthony hated his curls and on one occasion took a pair of scissors and started to cut, saying, "I hate these curlies!" And I found it interesting that, at about the same age, he was as happy to play with the pots and pans in the kitchen as he was his toys. By the same token, when I got him his first baby's potty, before he actually used it, he would put the bowl on his head as if it were a white bowler hat. No end to his ingenuity! He did like hats, and upon arriving home, he would put on one of his hats and go out the door saying, "I'm going to work." And for a little while he'd go over to the apartment of a neighbor who enjoyed his short visits.

When he was about four, he seemed to be hard of hearing; the pediatrician said he had tonsillitis and water by his eardrum and needed his tonsils and adenoids removed. When I brought him to the hospital and he was put in a hospital bed, he did not want to be there. When given a sleep-inducing injection, he fought it tooth and nail. He looked like a little bulldog, fighting sleep. Then, though, he was rewarded by a diet of popsicles and ice cream for a day or two, and improved hearing.

The recreation center offered swimming classes for children, and I enrolled him. As the kids gained proficiency in swimming, they were encouraged to jump off the diving boards and then to dive. The teacher told me that my son was fearless, and one day I watched him try to dive off the high board and end up in a belly flop. I can't imagine how much that must have stung, but he never complained about it.

Once, in a restaurant, he told me he needed to go to the bathroom, and as I got up to help him go (still in the ladies' room), I said out loud, "I guess he'll need to use the men's room on his own one of these days," and he walked right in to the men's room. On another occasion, when he was asleep in bed (I thought), I went outside to take five minutes to pick up milk at a market half a block down the street. As I was starting down the driveway in my car, Anthony ran out the door, screaming, "Mom! Mom!"

I stopped the car, got out and said, "Oh, Anthony, I'm so sorry! I didn't mean to scare you. I was just going to the corner to get some milk. Do you want to come with me?"

He said, "No, that's okay," and I put him back to bed. All of which goes to show that assuming that kids don't understand is an old wives' tale.

A friend of mine, Dan Gregory, contributed to the cost of getting Anthony's first two-wheeler bike, with training wheels, and I went to the school playground a half a block down the street and held the seat while he pedaled; however, it was his twin neighbors, Mitch and Mark Guzman, who actually got him riding solo. As I went to the school to see how it was going one day, I heard Anthony yelling, "Mitch! Cut it out! Stop, Mark!" After teaching him to actually ride alone, they proceeded to ride into him to get him to fall off. Being identical twins, they found numerous tricks to confound teachers, friends, and adults.

As I was not the most patient mother/role model, Anthony learned to get angry easily as well. And some kids liked to get him angry. However, his kindergarten and fourth grade teacher, Mr.

Schiff, told me that, at one time, some kids pulled him to the ground and tried to put a stick in his ear; however, he got up and pushed one of them down, and he didn't have any trouble after that. He was in the fourth grade then. But before that incident I was walking to his classroom when I saw some kids giving him a hard time, and he yelled after them, "You rubber dildo!"

At the time I didn't know what the word meant, but found out quickly.

These stories occurred when Anthony was at Wilson Elementary School, a block away, which was convenient. I worked part time at the school as a parent liaison for the Head Start Program; speaking Spanish, I could explain to Spanish-speaking parents what the program was about and how they could help their children in math and reading.

Anthony's final year at Wilson was the sixth grade, and the sixth grade teacher, who had taught there for decades, always taught sex education and did a good job with it, I thought. Better to teach the kids before puberty, before they have become self-conscious. She taught the boys separately from the girls, and she recommended a TV program that presented the material well, and that children and parents could watch together, as well as read some well-written books.

I remembered the time *I* was learning about sex. In the fourth grade, one of my precocious classmates, Marjorie Phyfe, took me aside one day and said, "Natalie, why don't you ask the teacher to tell us about the facts of life?"

"Okay," I answer nonchalantly; I went up to Mrs. Roth and asked, "Could you tell us about the facts of life?"

"Well, I don't know," she answered, reddening. "I would have to get permission from Miss Bishop."

Two weeks later: "Natalie, ask her again," said Marjorie.

"Did Miss Bishop say you could tell us about the facts of life?" No doubt she had been hoping we'd forget.

"I will plan to do it, but if there is any silliness, or laughing, I will stop immediately."

"Okay! Yay!" we said. And so Mrs. Roth gave it her best shot, and when she started to talk about intercourse, many of us had to stop from snickering, but we got through it, as did Mrs. Roth.

Since I told all this to my mother, she felt it was her responsibility to do the same, perhaps because, when my sister got married, she had written her a note saying that, although she had neglected to inform Carol about this issue, just to know that it took practice. And when she sat me down do her maternal duty—and she did draw very nice illustrations—she repeated, "But it really is a very beautiful thing." After all that, Anthony's sixth-grade teacher made it easy for the parents. And I can say, thankfully, that Anthony has, as far as I know, acted with good judgment in his romantic activities.

When we came to the teen-age years, it seemed that the minute Anthony set foot in his seventh-grade classroom, puberty infiltrated. The changing of the voice, the large feet forewarning a growth spurt, the outdoing his role model (mother) in the use of sarcasm, sometimes wit, the not wanting to be seen with his mother (which I thought was funny, having felt the same way myself about my own mother), the shouting "I hate you!" (which I didn't like but was glad he could say it, since I had felt the same way at times with my parents but wouldn't have dared to).

Anthony wasn't interested in studying, but he did like sports, and I was glad he liked *some* activity—we all need to like and care about something, and sports kept him on a positive path. When Anthony was going into the ninth grade at La Cumbre Junior High and looking forward to being top dog there, the Santa Barbara School District decided that the ninth grade should move to the high schools—San Marcos, Santa Barbara High School, and Dos Pueblos in Goleta—to the dismay of incoming ninth graders who would have to wait another four years before being on top. They were not happy about that.

Although Anthony would have gone to Santa Barbara High School since we were in that district, Larry wanted him to go to San Marcos because more of the parents worked in professional fields, and Larry thought that kind of exposure was important. I had no objections; although many of his neighborhood friends were going to SBHS, he would make new friends and still be able to see his old friends in our neighborhood. Further, he had already started with the football team, so, by the time school actually started, he had already gotten to know other players.

One of the activities I enjoyed was preparing the early dinners for the football team before their games. Each parent had a job. Two of the fathers barbecued tri-tips; one or two made and served the salad; another gave out the garlic bread; and I put a baked potato on each plate. There was milk or juice but no dessert.

Anthony had two very good friends who played football with him. Jonathon Pryor, about six feet eight (and later played for UCLA), had platinum-blond hair and a good-natured smile. Anthony dated his twin sister Catherine then, and they were the two youngest children of the Presbyterian minister, Rev. Robert Pryor.

Brian Pickett was short and quite black, had grown up in the Bronx, and had come to Santa Barbara with his mother. The contrast in their size, color, and shape was remarkable. Brian was the only Black student in the class, and a tiger in sports. On one occasion at a pre-game dinner, the guys were clambering to their places when suddenly Brian's voice rose: "All right, you guys, we're saying grace." And silence ensued while Brian blessed the meal.

Jonathon's mother, Mary-Lou, was everything I wasn't, and she made care packages and laundry bags for Anthony and Brian when they went to college, and sent cookies. I sent brownies to Anthony once, in a tin, but when they arrived, they were moldy.

But Anthony's main sports interest in high school became wrestling. His coach, Sam Razo, became a mentor to him. I went to the wrestling tournaments and to the end-of-year wrestling dinners, and there met the coach's mother as well.

Some form of award or appreciation was given to each student, and there was much camaraderie in the events. However, the first time I watched a wrestling match, I became seriously anxious. First I watched the guys warm up, which included their doing a backbend—not on their feet and hands, but on their feet and head! I was sure someone's neck would break, but no, and they developed nice thick necks. The lightweights always began the tournament, and those wrestlers were agile and fast, which created its own kind of intensity. Brian was in the lighter weight class, though not the lightest. It was a relief to see him win—but in the meantime, I noticed, on the opposing side, a young Black man wearing a hood, pacing, and eyeballing Anthony. That made me nervous. Then, looking at Anthony, I saw his face and body looking calm and relaxed, seemingly unaware of this threatening being. By then, though, I was literally grinding my teeth. And I was elated when Anthony pinned his opponent within a minute! I mentioned it to him later, and he replied, "That's just an intimidation tactic."

FOOTBALL GAMES ARE LIKE A COMMUNITY PICNIC. Wrestling matches are one-on-one and intense. And although injuries are not as prevalent as they are in other sports, there is the danger of getting cauliflower ears, and sometimes they get infected. Also there are the diets required to "make weight," consisting of grapefruit juice. I don't know if they are still legal, as some serious problems have ensued because of dehydration.

When Anthony was a junior, several branches of the military were recruiting juniors and seniors. There was a career center at the school, but it wasn't proactive in giving students a clear picture of types of jobs, incomes, proficiencies needed, etc., and so was overshadowed by the recruiters on campus.

Anthony's friend, Marco Rodriguez, knew he wanted to be a career marine. Anthony thought he'd like to join the marines and work on jets to make a good salary, for obvious reasons. He wanted to sign up, but Larry was strongly opposed, as he had had a taste of the marines when young and had difficulty with the strong type of discipline they espoused.

I was between Anthony and his dad. I didn't really want Anthony to join the marines, but felt that if that is what he wanted I shouldn't forbid him and make him resentful. So I told Anthony that I would approve it if that is what he wanted but we would not mention it to Larry. Anthony signed up, drove to Los Angles, and swore in, though, when the recruiter came to talk to me first, he said that there would be a penalty if Anthony then wanted out. I told him that I would give my approval, but if Anthony changed his mind, I would support him. I felt that there was too much pressure by the recruiters on the campus, and the threat of penalty angered me. I told Anthony that, if I went to jail, I'd write a lot of letters exposing intimidation tactics on the part of the marines, and I would not pay a large penalty.

As it turned out, the recruiters were getting bad publicity for pressuring students; Anthony did change his mind and went back to Los Angeles to swear out.

We then sent applications to California state colleges. San Marcos High School did very well in wrestling and was nicknamed "the Guillotine"; Anthony was called "the Chief Executioner"; needless to say, he was in demand by the colleges, and to stay on the team, he had to keep his grades up.

He decided to go to Humboldt State University, where the head wrestling coach helped him to get financial aid. This was fortunate, because, despite being an educator, I would not have been able to foot the bill. He received a Pell Grant and also was in a work-study program and spent time in Juvenile Hall, working with kids there, where, he said in describing one incident when a kid freaked out, "My wrestling came in handy." Being a wrestling coach and a school counselor is not a bad combination, and one of the classes he is qualified to teach, besides health (and sex education) is career planning, where students consider the kinds of jobs they might like and to find out what kind of income is offered, where they would like to live, and how much it would cost.

Although Anthony does not see his father frequently, I feel happy that Anthony has become the kind of role model that he missed out on having. On that side of the family, he is in touch with Uncle Frank, who when Anthony was in a high chair enjoyed feeding him peas!

I was glad that my son wasn't easily swayed. He and a friend, Bobby, did some yard work for a friend of mine on a few Saturdays. On one of the days Bobby called Anthony. While doing the dishes, I heard Anthony say, "No. No, no. No! *Noooo*," for quite a while.

"What did he want?"

"He wanted to skip the job today and go cruising" (in my car).

THE MIXER

I'm at a dance with my boyfriend, and they have a mixer.
The women line up opposite the men,
and we pair off at one end.

The partner I get was once at a singles meeting.
He argued with the discussion leader and,
when he was told to knock it off,
got mad and left.

He's wearing a clean shirt but smells like booze.
He really thinks he's cool,
doing a slow step, then pausing for a bit,
and then going into a few fast turns.

I feel like a pawn and don't like it.

Everyone else is having a good time dancing.
My boyfriend dances by and says the mixer's over.

Next mixer:
I get in line and look across at the men's line.
The creep's nowhere in sight, but
I'm ready to change my place if I see him opposite me.

The line moves down, and I keep checking across.
Any partner'd be a pleasure compared to him.

Two people leave. One.
Suddenly, there he is in front of me.
I'm taken so off guard I don't even think to walk away.
So I tolerate yet another miserable dance.

For the next whole week I'm mortified.
What was I doing to attract
the only drunk in the whole place?

I should not *be* attracting old men, drunks,
and losers; This guy *stalked* me!
What's worse—I didn't do a thing,
and that's the most upsetting thing of all.

I never want to be chosen again.
Some mixer.
I'll do the choosing from now on.

THE MUGGER

He grabs me from behind and pulls me to the ground.
He sits on my stomach,
pins my hands over my head,
and slaps my face.
I raise my elbow towards my face,
then raise my knee.
"Put that knee down."
"Okay."
He points his finger in front of my nose. "You wanna die?"
"No."
"Then do what I say, bitch."
"Okay." He slaps again.
I raise my knee and lift my hip.
As he rolls off, I shout, "No!"
And prepare to kick.

ANTHONY FRANCIS
CALIFANO (2)

WHEN I WAS TEACHING ESSENTIAL SKILLS at Santa Barbara City College, one of the classes that I enjoyed was a six-week writing class; students met for two hours twice a week, Most of them were in their twenties, coming back to the community college to catch up on what they had missed by not completing high school, or to start in college after taking a few years off after high school.

I told them, "Your words—and therefore your thoughts—are important and have validity," and as many of them didn't have access to a typewriter or word processor, I enjoyed typing up their stories and giving them back to read aloud to their partners in class or to have their partners read them back to them. Then we talked about what they had written, about their ideas, their organization, and the grammar.

One of the first assignments I gave them was to write about their lives in two parts: to describe where they were from age zero to eleven, what it was like; and then to identify three major events or influences during those years.

In reading these papers, I found something remarkable. Approximately eighty percent of these young people came from families that had gone through a divorce. They mentioned going through periods of turmoil, insecurity, and negativity. But in time their lives became more stable and they acquired a sense of direction and self-assurance.

Why did this strike me as so remarkable? I was a single parent raising my son under financial stress and time constraints. I felt guilty that Anthony was living in a home without a male role model and with a stressed mother.

The fact that he had found sports, especially wrestling, to give his life structure gave me hope that, in time, he would find his way, and in less time than it had taken me to find mine. He was living with me, also, while I was trying to catch up with the things I wanted to do when growing up, i.e., music and theater. I wanted to find a supportive mate/father image that we both would benefit from. I worried that the limits of his upbringing might be damaging to him.

More of that is material for another memoir, but the following are a few examples of some of our interchanges:

Anthony, age seven, when we are driving to deliver flyers for Children's Theater: "Where are we going?"

"To the Alpha School."

"Mom, I'm not going there! I'm not retarded!"

"No, Anthony, you're not. I'm not taking *you* there. I'm bringing the flyers to the school, so they can come to the children's show."

Parents' night at La Cumbre Junior High, we are going upstairs to one of the teacher's rooms. I am looking at the floor plan and saying, too loudly, apparently, "Is room twenty-three straight ahead or to the left?"

"Shut up, Mom!" I guess he didn't want to see his mother looking, acting, or talking like a dork. At least I wasn't wearing the pants he hated. He might not have gone if I had.

But then, one year he gave me a stuffed animal for Christmas. A raccoon. I still have it. He got angry once and pulled off its tail, but I sewed it back on. Another time he threw it in the garbage, but I retrieved it.

Or: My singing friend Joan was at my apartment practicing "Bosom Buddies" from *Mame*. Anthony, then in high school, came in during our practice. Joan called out, "Hi, Anthony! What do you think of our performance? Do you think we'll be on TV?"

"Sure—*The Gong Show*."

Or, about the same age, he tells me he's going out on a Friday night. "Where are you going?"

With a look of pure indignation at my audacity, he cries out, "None of your business!"

"Anthony. Until you are eighteen, I am your legal guardian. If anything happens to you, I need to know where you are. I am legally responsible for you."

With a tone of great irritation, he mutters, "Over to Tony's."

Anthony liked Dick Nelson because he thought he was a jock. Dick played catch with a football with him at one time, showing him how the real pros did it.

He liked Raoul because he talked to him a lot, once even offering to give him ten dollars for every "A" he got in school. Anthony went right into his room and started studying. I was not happy. Raoul didn't always follow through.

As for Dick Galway, Anthony's reaction wasn't enthusiastic, but he never said much about him until I broke up with Dick. When I told him, he said, "That's okay with me. I never did like him anyway." I had to admire the boy. He had the decency to keep quiet.

MARCH, 1989, SANTA BARBARA, CALIFORNIA: GETTING READY FOR THE MOVE

The truth is,
I'm at a loss.
I came unprepared.
My writing is either
in storage
or in the mail.
As the time gets closer
for me to leave,
I become more certain
that I want to
get back here.
But my father is there,
and he deserves consideration.
So does my financial status.
My kid would like
to take my car
before I'm ready to give it up.
I'll soon be in limbo—
in between.
I'd like to eat

everything in sight,
drink coffee all day,
and smoke a pack of cigarettes.

My Twenty-Five Years
In Santa Barbara, California

The weather's warm, the outdoors beckon;
clothing's casual.
I changed from a sheltered newlywed
of twenty-three
to a forty-nine-year-old divorcee,
singer, teacher;
I raised my son, kept going on
in sickness and in health,
on a small salary.
Some men wanted commitment
but didn't want to give it.
There were earthquakes,
oil spills, droughts, and fires
in this town with its aura of warm
"all's right with the world."
Now back in New Jersey where I grew up,
I miss my friends
and the warm sun.
Their visits are a gift.

SINGLES CAMPING TRIP—JIM

He's one of those interesting-looking men,
the intellectual, lumberjack type:
tall, hefty, salt-and-pepper beard,
intelligent blue-gray eyes.
He sits in a lawn chair,
plunks his brown-booted feet
on a fallen tree stump,
and says, "Oh, well, you can't do much
about the image, once it's there."
One friend said he would become aloof
and withdraw from relationships. She knew.
He said he saved some money
by quitting drinking,
and that he is used to living alone
in spite of having had
a few long-term relationships;
that he likes a place to himself,
even though
he's presently renting a room
from a lady friend
who is also independent.
Once in awhile, he gets on a talking jag—

one of those running monologues that go on
for hours and keep people in stitches.
He likes Shakespeare and knows a lot about geology;
He's not convinced it's worth it to work,
especially in Santa Barbara, where the money
doesn't go very far anyway.

WITHDRAWAL

Prickly forehead, drowsiness, headache.
I miss my coffee.
I went from seven to two cups a day,
and I'm in withdrawal!
A friend quit from seven cups, cold turkey, to zero!
She had no symptoms!

Once, after giving it up,
I had three Irish coffees.
I didn't even get high,
But by 5:00 a.m., after no sleep,
I figured I might as well get up and bake bread.

Do Americans use rest rooms
more than other cultures
because they drink so much coffee?
I wake up, go to the kitchen, and put on the water.
Those first few sips: the taste,
the little, warm zing—
Oh, what else is there like it?

TRANSITIONS

1.

Clara Martinez came up to me and said,
"Teacher, I may have to drop out of school.
My husband told me I could take classes
if I got the housework done.
But I don't know if I can. I'm getting
tired, and I can't always finish my housework
and my homework. I can't concentrate at home."
Goddammit, I thought. There goes
another waste of intelligence and talent.

2.

Taeko wanted to learn so badly.
She taught Japanese doll-making
and flower arranging in her country
and had an impressive resume.
Here, she was "allowed" to spend about
two hours a week at school, and didn't have time
to do her homework, because the house
had to be "ship-shape."
She came to this country
because she thought women could have more freedom here.
But her American husband liked the fact

that she was a polite, intelligent woman
with "traditional" training.
So she was in a bind.

3.
Cal dated a lot of women over a couple of decades.
Then he found a lovely young Philippino woman
through an out-of-country marriage service.
He went to the Phillippines and married Veronica,
brought her to Santa Barbara
and, shortly thereafter, to my E.S.L. class.
Veronica wrote a composition
about her marriage.
She was very much in love with Cal
and, since I knew him, invited me
to a lovely lunch at their home.
I had previously been to parties
at that charming, ranch-like place.

At lunch, Cal asked me,
in front of his loving wife,
if I had ever had sex
with more than one man at the same time.
I replied drily that I didn't have time
to think about such things,
being a single parent on a very small income.

What an S.O.B.

A year or two later, I saw Veronica walking
out of the News-Press Building
on De La Guerra Street.
We greeted each other with a hug and chatted.

"I'm working four hours a day here," she told me.
"Good for you! Congratulations," I said.
"And how's Cal?"

Her face fell.
"We separated and will probably get divorced."
"Oh, I'm so sorry."

"He was having affairs with other women,
and I just couldn't live with that."

That bastard, I thought. She adores him,
and he pulls this kind of shit. Damn him.
And she is proud of finding work for herself.
She still hopes he's proud of her. I can tell
from the way her face still lights up
when she talks about him.

How admirable of her to do what she did.
Fortunately, she told me, the local Quakers
supported her and found her another place to live.

AMAZING GRACE

There was a time when I was alone, sick, and in despair.
That time passed. I recovered.

Then, another time, I was sick but not alone.
My friends and neighbors gave me love and their support.

Yet again, twice, I had a crisis.
My life was hanging by a thread.
My neighbor took me to the ER.
Doctors treated me with skill.
The staff attended to my needs when I was helpless.
Friends called and helped.
Both times, it was twelve days before Christmas.
I see God's love.

REDEMPTION

One day twenty-two years ago,
I sat in my bathtub and sobbed
because everything in my life was wrong.
I was afraid I would crack and never recover.

Then, unable to function, I lay in the sun
and was soothed. I said to myself,
"I'll have to take one day at a time."

Today, after voice lessons, a child, a divorce,
three abortions, three alcoholic boyfriends,
single parenting on several part-time jobs
and a poverty budget,
music, theatre, colitis, psychotherapy,
a master's degree, Crohn's disease,
unemployment, and colon surgery,

I stood in my shower and looked out my bathroom window
and thanked God,
for today, I felt real joy.

NOVEMBER 18, 1988:
JUST LIKE MY MOM

A S DIRECTED, I STOOD ON A CHAIR, looked into the eyes of the man in front of me, put my right hand on the small of his back, took his right hand with my left, and started to sway to the music.

Oh, God, I thought. I'll never be able to stay for the whole workshop and sing tonight. I better tell Warren at the lunch break and just go home. "Did anyone ever tell you how absolutely gorgeous your eyes are?" I crooned, feeling like an absolute jerk.

"No, I don't think anyone ever has," he responded brightly.

Next, Warren asked the participants to divide—men on the stage, and women seated in the audience according to income, the highest earners in the front rows, the poorest in the back. Being on unemployment, I was the last one in the back. The men were told to take off their shirts, turn around, and pull their pants tight around the crotch. Then, turning back, they could make eye contact with the women and later ask them questions. The women were to choose a man to invite to lunch, foot the bill, and, on the way back to the workshop, try to kiss them.

On the way out, I saw one man standing by himself at the door.

"I'd really like to take you to lunch, but as you can tell, I've got laryngitis, and I have to go home," I apologized.

"Oh well, maybe some other time," he said politely.

AT HOME, I PLAYED MY ANSWERING MACHINE. My father's voice was the first message. "Nats, it's your old man. Your ma died this morning. Now, don't worry about trying to get here sooner. I'm all right, and next week will be soon enough."

Well, it had been expected. I made some tea and sat at the kitchen table. I thought back to the previous January; my mother had been in critical condition with pneumonia. She must not have wanted to die because she pulled through, and I was grateful to have been there for two months while she partially recovered. A special time, and although I would have liked to be there again, I felt that, if this was when Mom'd been ready to go, then it was all right. I thought of the time in the hospital when Mom had been wacky and eating Kleenex, and when the exasperated nurse had tried to reprimand her by saying, "Mrs. Beaumont, do you know the Lord?"

Without missing a beat, Mom had replied, "Well, not intimately, dear."

I put on some more water and got my vocalizing tape ready. I tried the first exercise. Nothing. I couldn't get a sound out.

I dialed the director of the dinner show and got her answering machine. "Elizabeth, this is Natalie. I don't think I can sing. I've got laryngitis," I rasped, and hung up.

How can I not sing? I have three solo numbers and four group numbers. If I don't show, I'll be wiping out one-fifth of the program. Singers were to arrive at 5:00. At 3:00 I tried to sing again. Nothing. More tea. More rest. At 4:00 I still couldn't get a croak out. I took a hot shower and put on some make-up base.

My mother died this morning, I observed. I can't sing, and I'm putting on my makeup to go to sing. That's what my mother would do.

I put on the rouge, then the eye shadow and lipstick, and powdered my face. I got dressed, remembering how my mother would always go to work when she had a bad cold, which sometimes developed into pneumonia. When pressed to stay home and rest, she would say, "I can't stay home. There are lives at stake!"

"What about *your* life, Mom?"

"Oh! I never thought of that!" she cheerfully answered.

I don't believe this. I am doing exactly what she always did.

There is a certain amount of humor in this. I can't sing, and I'm getting ready to sing in a dinner show. I put on my coat, got my keys, and drove over to the college. Inside, I saw Elizabeth, looking as if she were past caring.

"I left you a message. I've got laryngitis. I couldn't get a note out!"

"Sing over it," Elizabeth said wearily. "Whatever else goes wrong doesn't matter."

"Right."

I got through my first song somehow, but during the second I croaked on the highest note and sang the rest of the song an octave lower. When I got to the group numbers, I got through them thinly, but enough to get by. Feeling good about that and more relaxed, I went to Harry's Plaza Café with the group after the show for my customary piña colada, which felt pretty good, although all the time I was thinking about going in to sing when I couldn't, so typical of my mother. Well, I'd gotten the job done. I'd pulled it off. My mother would approve, and others would enjoy the similarity.

BREAKING UP WITH DICK

I beat myself up,
since I should have known better.
I did know better, but still,
he bought me back—not once, but twice—
giving me enough of what I wanted,
but always at a price.

Things'd be okay, but then
he'd pull the rug out.
I didn't get it, though;
didn't trust my instincts,
so I had to learn the hard way.

It was bizarre, warped,
twisted, horrible, insulting.
I made a mistake
and Dick needed to somehow get even.
He did.
Our time is dead, but its distorted ghost
hangs in the air and pops up now and then.

Oh, sure,
he's just a guy with charm,

and vulnerabilities, and fears,

like everybody else—
but to me he was the last straw
of something I don't want,
offering the hope of something I did.

SILENCE SITS AND SINGS

Silence

sits

and

sings

So

I see

stillness

in

myself

and

out

Stillness

spreads

Solace

saves

my hungry

soul,

my

spirit

About the Author

Natalie Beaumont was born in 1939, raised in Englewood, New Jersey, and attended the Dwight School for Girls from pre-primary until her high school graduation in 1957. She received a B.A. in French from St. Lawrence University in 1961. In the summer of 1960 she traveled to France and Switzerland through the Interchurch Center in New York City, spending the month of August working in the laundry of L'Hopital Continel, and allowing the regular employees to take their summer vacation.

She worked the summer after graduation, again through the Interchurch Center, painting front stoops in Harlem, New York, and living with Mrs. Alzenia Walsh next door to The Church of the Master on Morningside Drive, where Rev. James Robinson of Operation Crossroads had previously been pastor. In the fall of 1961, she was employed by St. Luke's Hospital as a case aide in the Social Service Department, where she met her husband-to-be, Larry Califano, who worked in Medical Records.

They married in March 1963 and moved to Santa Barbara, California, in October 1965, he to obtain his high school equivalency and an A.A. degree at Santa Barbara City College, and she to work in the business office of St. Francis Hospital.

In March 1967 their son, Anthony, was born; however, they divorced in 1969. Larry became a social worker for the Department of Welfare; Natalie began teaching English for the adult education program and, shortly thereafter, earned an adult education credential and a secondary teacher's credential from the University of California. She began teaching on the City College campus and in 1974 received a master's degree in Education with a reading specialist credential.

After her son was born, she also studied voice with Mrs. Lura Dolas and became active in Santa Barbara Playhouse–Plays for Children, serving as bookkeeper of that organization as well as performing in adult and children's theater.

Because full-time work was not forthcoming at the community college even after she earned her master's degree, she and another part-time instructor, on the advice of the Gray Panthers of Santa Barbara, organized and worked with the community college's instructors association to lobby for benefits and more job security. Although some inroads were made, Ms. Beaumont would not benefit, and in April 1989, when her son was at Humboldt State University, she returned to Englewood, after her mother's death, to help her father; as she put it, "Why work in a dinky job for a squat salary and a high rent, when you can live in a beautiful Victorian home rent-free and learn about the stock market?"

The Short Side of Paradise describes her life as a single parent during the twenty-five years she lived in Santa Barbara.